The Golden Years Ain't for Wimps

Karen O'Connor

HARVEST HOUSE PUBLISHERS

EUGENE, OREGON

Karen O'Connor: Published in association with the Books & Such Literary Agency, 52 Mission Circle, Suite 122, PMB 170, Santa Rosa, CA 95409-5370, www.booksandsuch.biz.

Cover by Dugan Design Group, Bloomington, Minnesota

THE GOLDEN YEARS AIN'T FOR WIMPS
Copyright © 2008 by Karen O'Connor
Published by Harvest House Publishers
Eugene, Oregon 97402
www.harvesthousepublishers.com

Library of Congress Cataloging-in-Publication Data
O'Connor, Karen
The golden years ain't for wimps / Karen O'Connor.
    p. cm.
ISBN-13: 978-0-7369-2247-0
ISBN-10: 0-7369-2247-4
1. Older Christians—Religious life. 2. Aging—Religious aspects—Christianity.
I. Title.
BV4580.O358 2008
248.8'5—dc22

                                                         2007036575

Printed in the United States of America

11 12 13 14 15 / BP-SK / 11 10 9 8 7 6

*To the men and women I've known
who have led the way to the happy golden years!*

Acknowledgments

I wish to thank these men and women for contributing their ideas, experiences, and story seeds—all of which have been woven into the fabric of this book in a creative way.

Charlotte Adelsperger • Bev Adler • Nicole Amsler • Betty Blyler • Janet Burr • Michele Buschman • Amy Canada • Sharon Norris Elliott • Marilou Flinkman • Charles Flowers • Kathleen Gibson • Margo Haren • Loralee Hunt • Patti Iverson • Susan Keck • Judith Larmon • Shirley Longlois • Patricia Lorenz • Brenda McKee • Brenda Nixon • Dympna Nuree • June O'Connor • Carrielynn Peace • Will Perkins • Marilyn Prasow • Sharon Riddle • Eileen Rife • Celeste Roberts • Jeneal Rogers • Laurie Russell • Mae Frances Sarratt • Joanne Schulte • Linda Evans Shepherd • Mike Smith • Jim Sweeney • Jan C. Thompson • Charlene Toomey • Mairin Torr • Shevawn Torr • June Varnum • Kathie Williams • Gary Winters • Jeanne Zornes

Contents

A Note from the Author

Oh those golden years! There are times when they glitter and times when they're a bit lackluster. Health problems, financial concerns, and relationship challenges can tarnish an otherwise happy day. On the other hand, we're generally confident in who we are, know how to enjoy life, have children and grandchildren to keep us young, and are wise enough to laugh at our foibles!

I hope the stories, scriptures, and prayers in this book will refresh you as you sit back, read, and smile in recognition of some of the funny and embarrassing moments that are part of these happy golden years we share. Of one thing we can be sure: God is with us in all of them—loving us, leading us, and even laughing with us as we travel the road of life here and hereafter.

Let us hold unswervingly to the hope we profess,
for he who promised is faithful.

HEBREWS 10:23

Karen O'Connor

It's All in a Word

Say It Again, Pam!

Barbara and Pam have been best friends since kindergarten. Today, at age 59, they're still finishing one another's sentences, just as they did when they were little girls.

"It used to make us laugh," said Barbara. "But at this stage of life it's become a necessity. What I can't recall, Pam does, and what she forgets, I remember. The other day we both had a 'mental pause' in my kitchen. And it almost led to an argument."

Barbara relived what happened. She remembered frowning in thought as the women visited over tea and blueberry scones. "Pam, what's the musical group that has an unusual name—like an animal, I think…"

Pam brightened. "The Animals."

"No, that's not it. It's the name of a specific animal."

Pam shook her head. "I don't know. I need more information."

Barbara leaned in. "Well, if I had more, I'd give it to you. Duh!"

Pam put her hands on her ample hips. "Hey, don't get huffy with me. You're the one who has the problem. I'm not concerned about some music group…"

"Well, if you're going to be that way about it, I won't say another word."

Pam picked up her keys and headed for the front door. "Good."

"Wait!" Barbara called. "I'm sorry. It's just that I heard this great song the other day, and it reminded me of the group. I think it was from the 70s. It brought back so many memories of high school."

Pam slipped her keys into her pocket and walked back into the kitchen. "What kind?"

"Romantic ones. It was about love."

Pam rolled her eyes. "Barbara, thousands of songs are about love. I need more to go on than that."

"Love and alive. Those are the only words I can remember. Darn! I wish I…"

"…could keep more than your name in your head?" Pam blocked Barbara's playful shove. They both laughed. "Hum a little. That might help," Pam suggested.

"I can't hum. You know that. Besides, I don't remember the tune." Barbara plopped down on a chair.

Pam leaned toward her. "Let me get this straight. You're trying to remember a group of musicians who have an animal's name, but it's not The Animals. A song you heard reminded you of this group, whose name you don't know, and it gave you a romantic memory, but you don't know the tune?" She let out a long breath.

"I know it's crazy. Is this what heading for 60 is about? I'm depressed already."

"When was this anonymous group popular?" Pam asked, ignoring Barbara's remark about her age.

"Seventies, I think. But they're still touring—or at least recording, as far as I can tell."

Pam looked at the ceiling. "Lord, keep our love alive, will you? We're about to crash and burn."

"Oh my! I think I've got it." Barbara leaped up. "That's it. Thank you. 'Love Will Keep Us Alive.'"

"That's not an animal name."

Barbara shook her head. Pam could be so annoying at times. "It's the name of the song, not the group."

Pam frowned. "The only group I remember from that long ago is the Eagles. They were my favorite musical group and still are."

"Pam, that's it!" Barbara jumped up and hugged her friend. "You saved me from waking up in the middle of the night and calling you when it popped into my head."

"Saved you? I think I saved myself a good night's sleep." Pam stood up and reached over to pat Barbara's hand. "Gotta run. But wait, an eagle is a bird. Why didn't you say bird in the first place, and we could have saved ourselves all this nonsense?"

Pam pulled her keys from her pocket, waved, and sauntered toward the front door.

Barbara picked up a pot from the stove. "I feel like bopping you over the head with this, but I need you and you need me—especially now that we're pushing 60 and our memories aren't what they used to be. At least yours isn't."

Reflection

Arise, LORD! Lift up your hand, O God.
Do not forget the helpless (Psalm 10:12).

———————————

Lord, how quickly I can head off a big problem when I turn to you first. But I usually do it second or third. I'm such a know-it-all sometimes! Even when I don't know it all—or even a little bit—I act as if I do. Thank you for bearing with me and reminding me that I not only need the help of a close friend but most of all your help in everything I think, say, and do.

Prostrate Prone

Marion is not only hard of hearing, she's not much of a speller either. As she's quick to admit, "Words cause me more than a little trouble."

Her sister Rona nods in agreement. "She confuses words that have similar spellings, and not hearing well adds to the confusion." But the women have a good attitude and a sense of humor.

Marion explained that she and her sister have enjoyed a weekly phone conversation every Sunday afternoon for 50 years. They started the tradition when they were young mothers and looked to one another for support during their parenting years. After the kids were grown they kept right on talking week after week, year after year, right into their 70s. The topics changed as the seasons of life came and went: raising kids, caring for elderly parents, dealing with midlife crises, marriage, hobbies, travel—and a bit of gossip once in a while.

In recent years their chats have more to do with the aches and pains of aging, their crossword puzzles, flower gardens, favorite movies, and husbands who aren't as much fun as they used to be.

On a recent Sunday afternoon Rona called Marion to complain. Her husband, Les, was turning into a couch potato and she was upset about it. "He won't take a walk with me anymore. Says his hips hurt too much."

"His lips hurt? What's that got to do with walking?" Marion asked. "Tell him lips are for kissing!" She laughed at her own wit.

Rona brushed off the mistake and kept on going. "It's as if he's given up on life...and on me. He's becoming prostrate prone."

Marion was suddenly quiet. She sniffled. "Rona, dear, I'm so sorry to hear about Les. He's always been so healthy and vibrant. But I guess trouble with—you know—one's private parts are common in men over 70. Let's just hope and pray that dear Les will live a long life despite his problems with you know what."

By this time Rona was confused. She held the phone away from her ear for a moment and took a deep breath—one she didn't want Marion to hear. She felt absolutely frustrated. First her husband began to shrink from life, and now it seemed her sister and best friend was doing the same thing. She couldn't make sense of Marion's comments so it seemed best to ignore them.

She blew a kiss into the phone and said, "I love you," as she had done every week for years and then added, "Gotta run. Talk to you next Sunday."

"Sure thing, honey," Marion agreed. "I look forward to it. And I'll send Les a card. You can count on it. Poor dear."

The following Wednesday an envelope addressed to Les arrived in the mail. Rona handed it to her husband at lunch. He slit it open and pulled out a get well card from Marion.

"What have you been telling your sister?" he asked.

Rona could tell he was miffed.

"Nothing important—just that you're not walking with me like you used to and I miss your company. I joked that you've become prostrate prone."

Les burst out laughing. "Well, I'll be," he shouted. "Marion's going to have to give in and get hearing aids." He handed the card to his wife.

She read it aloud.

Dear Les, please get well soon. I heard from Rona that you're prone to prostate problems. I remember your daddy had something similar. We'll be praying for you. Remember, God loves you and so do I.

Love, Marion

Reflection

I can do everything through him who
gives me strength (Philippians 4:13).

Lord, there is plenty to cry about during the golden years, so it's good when I find something to laugh at, even when it could be serious. Thank you for helping to tilt my glasses so I see the funny side of life too.

The Exhausted King

Harvey had gotten hearing aids, but he doubted they were doing their job. His wife tugged on his shirtsleeve and whispered in his ear more often than he wanted to admit. It seemed he was confusing words, mishearing initial sounds, and generally "missing the boat," especially when there were more than three or four people talking. About the only place he felt confident was in the first row of St. Andrew's Presbyterian Church, where he'd been a faithful member for more than 50 years.

But there was another problem—one Harvey was equally bummed about. He had a difficult time staying awake during Pastor Richard's sermons. He wished he could sit in the back so the minister wouldn't notice, but if he did he couldn't hear as well. On the other hand, if he snoozed he'd miss part of the sermon anyway—so what difference did it make where he sat? Harvey had a dilemma. He decided to put off his decision and spend the next few weeks sitting on the side near the worship group.

The following Sunday Harvey and Mabel arrived ten minutes before the service began. They chose two seats on the right side. Leonard Fuchs, the choir director, came into the sanctuary and took his place in front of the singers. Harvey leaned back and allowed the music to waft over him, filling his spirit with peace and joy and the love of the Lord.

He felt so good that he didn't care what happened next. He was already in ecstasy. He felt himself nod off a couple of times, but he pulled himself back to reality when the music swelled.

After the service he and Mabel walked out to the vestibule, greeted their friends, shook hands with Pastor Richard, and strolled out to their car in the corner of the parking lot.

Harvey tucked his hand in Mabel's and gave it a playful squeeze. "I loved the music today, didn't you? I felt as though I were sleeping on a cloud."

"It wasn't a cloud, dear. It was a seat—in church. And you not only snoozed, you snored. So I'm surprised you even heard the music at all."

Harvey dropped his wife's hand. "Not true," he growled. "I heard every word. I even know the title. It was my favorite song."

Mabel looked at him out of the side of her eyes. "And what might that title be?" she asked with a bite in her voice.

" 'The King Is Exhausted on High.' So there!"

Mabel breathed deeply. "The correct title, dear, is 'The King Is *Exalted* on High,' not 'Exhausted.' You're the one who was exhausted, Harvey, not the Lord."

Reflection

Come to me, all you who are weary and burdened,
and I will give you rest (Matthew 11:28).

Lord, I don't know about you, but I feel exhausted some-times—mostly of my own doing. I take on too much, worry too much, and meddle too much. It's time for me to take a break from other people's business, and my own too, and just focus my attention on you, the author and finisher of all things.

A Taxing Affair

April 15 was around the corner—and Hugh and Holly were in a dither. It was time to prepare their income tax forms and both dreaded the task. Holly had urged Hugh for the last few years to hire a financial manager so they wouldn't have to deal with this nonsense. Neither of them was good at filling out the paperwork, and it was taking a toll on their otherwise sweet relationship.

Hugh, however, was determined to see it through. "I don't want anyone poking into our affairs," he said. "Religion, politics, money—private!" And that was that.

He sat down on Thursday night, the week before the due date, and pulled out the file. He barked orders to Holly to bring him what he couldn't find, to sharpen his pencil, and to keep the coffee percolating. He was sure he'd be up well past midnight the way things were going.

Holly, on the other hand, felt grateful just to be alive and well enough at their ages, 74 and 76, to enjoy life in the United States and to experience all the freedom this afforded them. "Hugh, think about it. We have everything we need! We can move about as we please. We have the Lord in our lives, healthy, happy children and grandchildren, good neighbors, a church home, and a way of life that is ours today because of a lot of sacrifice and foresight on the part of our founding fathers. Just think, in the old country people were taxed without representation."

She barely got the words out of her mouth, when Hugh piped up, waving a handful of papers, "Well, taxation *with* representation isn't that hot either."

Holly burst out laughing. Hugh finally laughed too. Then Holly pulled up a chair beside her husband, tossed up a prayer of thanksgiving, and the two set to work on their taxes. They had a deadline to meet.

Reflection

Give everyone what you owe him: If you owe taxes,
pay taxes; if revenue, then revenue; if respect, then
respect; if honor, then honor (Romans 13:7).

Lord God, taxes are taxing. But if I simply follow your mandate to give to Caesar the things that are Caesar's and to you the things that are yours, I will be fine. Please help me do that today.

Emergency

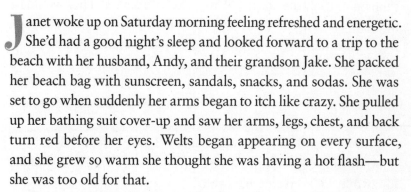

J anet woke up on Saturday morning feeling refreshed and energetic. She'd had a good night's sleep and looked forward to a trip to the beach with her husband, Andy, and their grandson Jake. She packed her beach bag with sunscreen, sandals, snacks, and sodas. She was set to go when suddenly her arms began to itch like crazy. She pulled up her bathing suit cover-up and saw her arms, legs, chest, and back turn red before her eyes. Welts began appearing on every surface, and she grew so warm she thought she was having a hot flash—but she was too old for that.

She jumped into the shower, hoping a dose of cold water would reverse the process, but it didn't make any difference. She dried herself off and slipped into something cool. Then she approached her husband and said, "Honey, something frightening is going on. Look at me. I'm a mass of red bumps, and I'm hot as an iron."

"My lands!" he shouted. "What is going on? We'd better get you to urgent care right away. Looks as if our day at the beach is going to be a day at the doctor's instead."

Janet let out a deep sigh. She was so disappointed. And how would Jake feel? He had so looked forward to their time together.

As she reached for the phone to call him with the news, Andy motioned her aside. She hung up the receiver before the line connected. "What's up?" she asked.

"I'm noticing your legs and arms. They're pink now, not red, and the welts are going down. Must be something you ate."

"But I had the same breakfast you did," she asserted. "I've never had such a reaction before to oatmeal and eggs."

"What about vitamins? Let's check the bottles. Maybe you took an overdose of something."

Janet waved her hand in the air. "That's ridiculous. I've had the same routine for years."

"Wait! Look at these two bottles—same shape, same manufacturer, just different colored labels. One's acidophilus and one's time-release niacin." He held them up. "I bet you took these by mistake," he said, pointing to the niacin. "Time release. That's it. They would be flushing your system about now—a couple of hours after you took them. How many did you take? One is the recommended dose."

Janet couldn't believe she'd made such a silly mistake. She opened both bottles and compared the color of the tablets. One was white and one was off-white—so close that in a hurry she wouldn't have noticed.

"Am I going to die?" she questioned. "I took a double dose."

Andy laughed and patted her hand. "No, but you might be flushing for awhile. I'll keep an eye on you."

Janet picked up the phone. "Jake, we'll be over in ten minutes. Gramma had a minor setback, but I'm going to live. I'll explain when we see you."

Reflection

Know that the LORD is God (Psalm 100:3).

Lord, you must get a kick out of me more than I'd like to admit. I do so many silly, unpredictable things, especially when I'm in a hurry. But you don't embarrass me. You simply save me from myself. For that I thank you with a full heart.

Cracking the Code

"Lyle, dear, I can't find the thingamajig that goes with the whatcha-macallit. Any idea where you put it?"

Lyle walked into the guest bathroom, scratching his head. "The thingamajig? What the heck is that?"

Ellie's look pinned her husband to the tile wall. "What do you mean you don't know? You're the one who had it last."

Lyle crossed his arms in front of his chest. "Did not."

Ellie crossed hers. "Did too." She took a breath and stretched out her words. "Let me start over. You know," she continued, uncrossing her arms and flailing them in front of Lyle's face, "you came in from that store—you know that whozywhatsit place where you bought the whateveryoucallit thingy for this bathroom. Renae called this morning. She wants to buy one just like it. I told her I'd ask you the price and if there was a choice of color." Ellie stood her ground and didn't flinch.

"Look, dear, I can't help you if I don't know what you're talking about. I bought a bunch of supplies at the diddleywhatsit place, and then I stopped by the—you know the store that makes me think of trains."

Ellie blinked and knitted her brows. "The place that makes you think of trains?"

"Hmmm." Lyle appeared determined to save face. He raised his voice. "It's a store that sells stuff for people that like to do—you know—projects, stuff that helps with gardening and plumbing and lighting and painting."

"And that kind of a store reminds you of trains? Do they sell miniature train sets?"

"No!" Lyle's face turned red. "They don't sell trains. It just reminds me of trains. You know, the place where a train goes after it's finished with its run."

"A train garage?" Ellie decided to try and help her husband, but she hadn't a clue where all this was leading.

"Warm, but not hot," said Lyle, egging her on with his fingers. "Keep going. You're almost there."

"What is this—a treasure hunt?" Ellie fanned her face with a hand. She had no idea how they got into this corner. There seemed to be no way out. "A train shed?"

"No, but you're getting there, I think."

"A depot—a train depot!"

"That's it!" Lyle crushed Ellie to his chest. "You're a genius. Now I can get a good night's sleep."

"But it's only ten in the morning." Ellie collapsed in her recliner. She had forgotten how all this started, and it didn't matter anymore. Her husband needed her. He was clearly on the precipice of a mental breakdown.

Lyle threw up his hands. "Home Depot!" he shouted. "Get it? *Depot!*"

Ellie sighed. She was relieved, but not amused. Lyle would be okay—at least for the moment.

"Now, back to our initial conversation," she said, lips pursed. "The one about that thingamajig that goes with the whatchamacallit. Any idea where you put it?"

"Not a clue, but if we go back to the Depot and walk up and down the aisles I'm sure we'll find what we're looking for. It's bound to be there somewhere. If it has to do with bathrooms, we'll check every doodad in every aisle until we find the hottle-dee-hoo. What do you say?"

"I say let's go. The train is waiting."

Reflection

Forget the former things;
do not dwell on the past (Isaiah 43:18).

Lord, thank you that even my whodlewhatsit prayers make sense to you. You are never confused by my conversations. I am so relieved to know that the Holy Spirit intercedes for me when I can't find the words I want to say.

Healthy Living

Doin' What Comes Naturally!

Flaxseed oil for proper assimilation, fiber for elimination, chlorophyll for heartburn, and calcium for strong bones...and so on. Al doesn't like it one bit, especially when his wife pounds her drum about what he should and shouldn't be eating during these golden years so they can enjoy a long and carefree life together.

"Don't you know we're all going to die someday?" he asked Elsa one sunny morning over the top of the daily newspaper. "Seems to me all these folks eating natural foods die of natural causes." He chuckled at his own wit and turned to his wife. "After all that pampering and figuring and watching and calculating about what you put into your mouth, you still die—just takes the health nuts longer than us folks who like to 'live' a little—if you know what I mean."

Elsa knew what he meant, all right. She'd been speaking her piece for nearly 50 years, and for the same amount of time Al had been speaking his—and the two never did meet. But they didn't part company either. They stuck it out—partly to honor God's will for marriage and partly to see how it would turn out. Elsa was certain Al would come around to her way of thinking, and Al was just as sure Elsa would come around to his.

That evening the conversation continued. It gave them something to talk and spar about as they faced each other over the dining room table—she with her poached salmon and wilted greens with a touch of citrus; he with a double cheeseburger and a side of fries.

The next night as they embarked on their daily ritual of prayer over the meal and conversation about the day, something came over Elsa. She teared up. She didn't know what the salty blobs were all about, but there they were, dripping onto her baked potato as Al looked on, his chicken-fried steak turning cold under his fork.

"Honey," Elsa said, "I'm suddenly realizing we probably don't have much time left, but whatever time we do have, let's finish well, shall we?"

Al dabbed at his eyes as she continued.

"Let's make a pact with each other and a deal with God," she continued. "Let's always be kind to one another from this day forward—regardless of our differences…and especially when we goof up, repeat stuff, forget names, or tell the same stories over and over—and even if we never agree on what to eat. If we aren't kind to each other, who will be?"

Al blotted his eyes with a corner of his blue-and-white cotton napkin and sniffed right over his side dish of macaroni and cheese. "You're right," he squeaked between the tears that flooded down his face and the moisture in his throat.

Then he smiled and reached for Elsa's hand. "Done deal," he said. "And I know the secret to stickin' to it."

Elsa's eyes widened. "You do?"

"It's the forgotten beatitude," he said, hiding a smile behind his hand. "Blessed are we who can laugh at ourselves for we never cease to be amused."

Elsa laughed out loud. "And if we keep that one," she said, "neither of us will ever be abused."

Reflection

And this is my prayer: that your love may
abound more and more in knowledge and
depth of insight...(Philippians 1:9).

---

*Lord, sometimes laughing at myself is just too much to ask,
but when I finally do it feels so good. Better I should take
the lead than someone else, right? What is the point of taking
life so seriously? I don't need to prove my point, just point
instead to you and ask your blessing on my day.*

Coffee, Anyone?

Nonie loved coffee, but coffee didn't love her. In fact it gave her cramps. The acid content was a bit much for her stomach. Since her reaction on some days was better than on others, she took her chances. She couldn't help but indulge. Nonie loved the aroma, the deep color, and the curl of steam rising over her favorite cup of brew. With a bit of honey and a splash of half and half, she was in heaven.

Nonie's daughter Laurie had a decidedly different opinion of coffee—especially when it came to her 83-year-old mother. She had spoken to her mom over and over about this coffee addiction and the fact that she, Laurie, was the one to rush over to her mother's apartment with antacid pills whenever Nonie had one cup too many.

Laurie decided to take matters into her own hands. For Mother's Day she purchased a beautiful pink Brown Betty teapot, a matching set of cups, and a basket of assorted herbal teas: chamomile, Lotus Blossom, Red Zinger, and, most important, Echinacea Wellness tea.

"Mom, I want you to promise me you'll try to exchange the coffee habit for the tea habit." Then Laurie launched into a lecture on the merits of the various selections. "Chamomile before bed assures a sweet sleep, and Echinacea Wellness will support your immune system and all-around good health."

Nonie listened patiently but Laurie could tell her mother was not buying her spiel. She'd always been stubborn, and she didn't appear to be any less so as she grew older.

The next time the two visited, they sat in the den—Nonie in her favorite recliner, and Laurie on the sofa across the room.

"Mom, how are you feeling? Any better?"

Nonie clutched her stomach. "Fair."

Laurie let out a deep breath and faced her mother eye-to-eye. "Are you still drinking coffee?" she asked. "After all I've told you and after I went to the trouble of buying you a beautiful teapot and cups and selecting delicious teas that will actually help you feel better?"

Nonie lowered her head. "Yes. I can't break the habit. When I go too long without a cup I get this terrible headache."

"And when you drink it, you get a stomachache. Which is worse?"

Nonie closed her eyes and rested her head against the chair.

Laurie stood up and paced the room. "Mom, this cannot go on! What am I going to do with you?" She thought for a moment and then tried a new tactic. "Mother, what do you think God wants you to do about this addiction that is hurting your body, which is his temple?" Laurie was sure she was on to something that would work. She knew how much her mother loved the Lord and that she wanted to please him above anyone else. "I think we should pray about this together and read God's Word for guidance."

Laurie reached for her mother's Bible on the bookshelf above the sofa.

Nonie raised her hand. "I've already done all that," she said. "I'm sure the Lord is fine with me drinking coffee. There is nothing in the Bible against it."

Laurie sighed. She was sure her mother was right. She couldn't imagine there being any reference to coffee in God's Word. But that wasn't the point. She wanted to focus on helping her mother pray for wisdom and strength so she could give up what was clearly not working.

Nonie stood up, walked to the sofa, and plucked the Bible out of Laurie's hands. She turned quickly to the New Testament and then lay the book open to the page she'd looked for.

"The Bible doesn't say anything against coffee," she said. "But it does seem to refer to it in a positive way."

Laurie frowned. She feared her mother was losing it.

"It's right here," said Nonie. "*He brews.*"

Reflection

Surely you desire truth in the inner parts; you
teach me wisdom in the inmost place (Psalm 51:6).

———————————

Lord, what fun to play with words and know you enjoy my sense of humor!

Chapped Lips

One thing Mary Ann did not like about living in Fargo, North Dakota, was the bitter cold that chilled her to the bone. She especially didn't appreciate going through the winter months with chapped lips. But she found a way to cope with it. She applied lip balm every morning under and over her lipstick, and she carried an extra stick in her purse or pocket.

One Friday morning she took a day off from work to drive her mother to the doctor's and to do a bit of Christmas shopping before the crowds descended on the nearby West Acres Shopping Center. The temperature was below freezing that day so she decided to skip the usual makeup. She was going to hurry in and out of the stores and didn't think she'd run into anyone she knew. Her friends were at work or home on a day like this.

Mary Ann ran a comb through her hair, pulled on a cozy pair of fleece pants and a red wool sweater, wrapped a heavy plaid scarf around her neck, and dug her arms into her down jacket.

"Nearly forgot," she said, as she grabbed her keys and walked toward the garage. "Lip balm, lip balm, especially on a freezing day like this."

Mary Ann took the tube out of her purse and smoothed it over her chapped lips. It felt so soothing she smeared a thick layer on the skin above and below her mouth as well. The last thing she wanted was chafed skin on top of chapped lips. She added a dab of lipstick to add some color so she wouldn't appear pale. There! She was all set.

Twenty minutes later Mary Ann walked into Macy's Department Store and strolled through the women's shoe department on the first floor. She pulled on a slider here and a boot there, and walked back and forth in front of the foot mirror to see how she looked. She hadn't purchased a new pair of shoes in over a year. It was definitely time for this 60-something woman to indulge herself. *Time to get with it!* she thought.

Suddenly she felt funny inside. Was someone staring at her? She whirled around and noticed a little boy pulling on his mother's jacket and pointing at her.

Two women sitting across from her looked up and then turned away chuckling. Mary Ann let out a deep breath. People could be so rude. Okay, maybe she didn't look too classy in her fleece pants and hooded down jacket, but at least she was warm and comfortable. Besides, what business was it of theirs how she dressed? This was a free country, and she could dress however she wanted. So there!

Still, Mary Ann felt self-conscious, and it only got worse as more and more people stared and then turned away or shook their heads and nodded—as if she were a freak.

Finally she couldn't stand it another minute. She wondered if apricot jam had caught in her front teeth or if coffee stained the front of her jacket. She headed for the women's restroom. She'd check herself out in the full-length mirror just in case. She pushed open the door and ran to the mirror across from the row of sinks.

When she took a gander at herself she nearly fainted. She looked like a clown! Her lips and skin around her mouth were smeared with bright-red shiny goo. *What is this?* she wondered. Then it hit her. Lip balm. She reached into the pocket of her purse and pulled out the tube. *Cherry Red. Oh no!* She had purchased it at the grocery store when she was in a hurry and had never glanced at the color.

She was red from the lip balm and pink from the lipstick. What a mess!

Oh for the good old days when lip balm was colorless. Mary Ann didn't need Mint Green or Blue Berry or Cherry Red. All she wanted for her poor chapped lips was plain, invisible lip balm.

Reflection

The LORD sustains the humble... (Psalm 147:6).

Dear God, rarely do I see myself as others see me. Good thing you see me as I truly am and are pleased with me just that way. Whew! Thank you for loving me.

Hear! Hear!

"Say that again."

"Didn't get it."

"Speak up."

It got so bad around the Jones' household that Maggie couldn't stand it another minute. "Conner, you've got to get hearing aids. This dilemma is interfering with our marriage. I can't spend the next decade repeating everything I say. I'll go insane! Do you hear me?" *Oh nuts! You can't hear me. That's the problem.*

Maggie wrung her hands and walked into the kitchen. She pulled out sugar and flour and butter and pecans and a baking pan. She turned on the oven, tied an apron around her middle, and opened her cookbook. She'd do what she always did when she and Conner were at a crossroads: Bake! A pie, some cookies, a dozen cupcakes made her feel better.

The doorbell rang just as she set her first batch of goodies on the granite counter to cool. Their neighbors Abby and Ray had stopped by to say hi.

"Come in. You're just in time to enjoy a slice of pie and some butter pecan cookies. How about some coffee or a cup of tea?" Maggie turned toward Conner sitting in his favorite chair with the TV blaring. "Honey," she shouted, "look who's here."

"What? Say it again!"

Maggie let out a deep breath. She turned to their friends. "See what I mean? It's getting worse by the day, and he doesn't seem to realize it."

Ray walked over and patted Conner on the shoulder. "We're here to visit. Come join us."

Conner stood up and smiled. He pumped Ray's hand and welcomed Abby too.

The four sat down for dessert.

Ray opened the conversation. "Con, Maggie tells us you're thinking about getting hearing aids. Good idea. I'll be looking into them in a few years myself." He laughed and looked around for approval.

Conner sat with a straight face. "I don't know what you're talking about. I'm fine. Can hear as good as anyone."

Ray backed down and then took a new direction. "I agree. Why would you need those things anyway? They're a nuisance, and they cost an arm and a leg. Besides, why would any man want hearing aids? If you stay hard of hearing you won't have to listen to your wife. Hardy-har-har." He thought it was funny. Abby and Maggie did not.

Conner saved the day. "I'd never stay hard of hearing for that reason," he said. "I'd miss hearing Maggie say, 'I love you,' just before we drop off to sleep. Funny how I never miss that one—no matter what."

Reflection

Hear my cry, O God;
listen to my prayer (Psalm 61:1).

Thank you, Lord, for hearing my every word and for speaking to me in such a way that I can hear every word you say.

My Achin' Back

Rita dialed her mother-in-law's phone number. When Carla answered, Rita told her she'd pick her up for church in 15 minutes.

"Honey, my back is acting up again. Would you mind coming a few minutes early and rubbing some of my ointment on the sore spots? I want to be able to pay attention when Pastor Hank gives his sermon."

"Glad to," Rita replied. "See you in a few."

Rita walked into Carla's home minutes later and applied the soothing cream.

Carla stood up and placed her hands on the small of her back. "A miracle! I feel so much better. Thank you, dear."

Rita smiled. She loved doing small favors for this great lady who was so generous with everyone.

They got into the car and Rita drove to church. They found their usual seats in the second row from the front, so Carla could hear without straining.

Midway through the sermon, Rita's right eye was itchy so she rubbed it vigorously with her right index finger. Suddenly she was in pain—real pain. No amount of rubbing made a difference. In fact it made it worse. *What's going on?* she wondered. Her eye had been fine minutes before.

Then it dawned on Rita that she'd neglected to wash her hands after using the ointment on her mother-in-law's back. It was clearly not meant for eyes! Tears streamed down her face. She slipped out of the pew and walked to the restroom, hoping cold water would ease the inflammation. She dabbed her eye with a wet paper towel and the sting lessened. She walked back into the sanctuary and slid in next to her mother-in-law.

Afterward, as the two drove home, Carla looked at Rita. "My dear, I don't think I've ever seen you so moved by Pastor Hank's preaching as I did this morning. I must be missing something. What is it? First you cried and then you sat up and stared straight ahead taking in every word. Why even your eyes were red with emotion."

Reflection

I am the LORD, who heals you (Exodus 15:26).

———————

Lord, thank you for being the healing balm in my life. Whenever I'm hurting you are here to soothe and comfort me.

Down for 20

B arney liked to take a 20-minute nap every afternoon. "Gonna put it down for 20," he'd call to his wife, Roberta, and then mosey on down the hall to the den where his recliner sat in the corner of the room.

If Roberta needled him about it, he just winked at her, patted her on the backside, and gave her the usual spiel: "Keeps me young and spunky!" Barney also believed a short snooze each day kept him in good health and in a good mood.

When he turned 75, Roberta held a small luncheon for him, complete with his favorite meal—linguini and clams, coleslaw salad with pineapple chunks, and chocolate mousse cake with plenty of chocolate and plenty of mousse.

Barney and Roberta's neighbors Shelly and Wes joined them, and Barney's former business partner Dick and his wife, Babs, came too.

After the meal and dessert, Roberta served tea while Barney opened gag gifts and funny cards. Shelly and Wes gave him a jar of bath salts for soaking his "tired ol' rear," which brought quite a laugh, and Dick and Babs gave him a card that said they'd bought him a gift—*The Memory Book: The Classic Guide to Improving Your*

Memory at Work, at School, and at Play—but couldn't remember where they'd put it!

"As soon as we run across it, we'll bring it over," Babs assured Barney.

Roberta was the last one to hand over a gift. Barney opened the card, which read: "Now that you're 75, live it up! Take *two* naps...and then you'll be in fine shape to join me for the jazz concert at Adams Hall on Friday night."

Barney thanked everyone, kissed Roberta on the tip of her nose, and after a bit of conversation, yawned, waved to everyone, and padded down the hall, calling over his shoulder, "Gonna put it down for 20."

Reflection

The sleep of a laborer is sweet (Ecclesiastes 5:12).

———————————

Dear God, there's nothing as nice as a nap when I'm all tuckered out. Ah, sweet sleep. Thank you for providing the rest I need and for nudging me to take it.

Body Beautiful

Chinny Chin Chin

Gail leaned in toward the hand mirror and looked at her face. She turned it over to the magnifying side. A little better, but it was still hard to see as close as she wanted to. And she really wanted to see up close now that she was prone to a brand-new condition she wasn't prepared for.

The hair that used to be on her legs had suddenly sprouted on her chin...and some of the little buggers were black and curly, even though the hair on her head was more white than gray. Her granddaughter Queenie had alerted her to the malady one autumn day when the two were having a picnic in the backyard. As Gail cut the peanut butter and jelly sandwiches into little squares and placed them in front of the four-year-old, Queenie piped up in a loud voice. "Grams, why do you have a black curl on your chin? Mom doesn't have one."

Gail ran a finger over her chin where Queenie pointed and sure enough, something pointy was sticking out of her smooth skin. She ran inside, grabbed a hand mirror, and inspected her face inch by inch. There it was. A black curly hair jutting straight out. Gail wondered how long it had been there. How had she missed it? Had the clerk at the grocery store noticed? Did the sight of it turn her husband away? Did her best friend, Ruth, laugh behind her back? She imagined the worst.

Gail fished for her tweezers and pulled that puppy out by its black tail and tossed it into the trash. She couldn't eat a bite till it was out of her life.

Just when she'd started enjoying the fact that she wouldn't have to shave her legs or underarms but once every couple of months, here she was on the verge of growing a beard. Next thing she knew she might be borrowing her husband's razor.

Gail dragged herself back to the picnic table, and she and Queenie ate their sandwiches. But Gail's mind was elsewhere. She couldn't stop thinking about the potential invasion of black hairs on her white chin. She considered electrolysis. Painful procedure, she'd heard, but it was now or never when it came to the invaders. Get 'em while she still had control. Like weeds in the garden, one can't wait too long or they take over the flowerbed.

"Grams?" Queenie interrupted Gail's thoughts. "What are you thinking about? You look sad."

Gail patted her granddaughter's soft hand. "It's hard to get old, honey. First the wrinkles land and now the black hairs pop out. And worst of all, I didn't notice them till you told me."

Queenie climbed off the picnic bench and tucked her little body next to her grandmother's on the other side of the table. She petted Gail's face and looked at her with soulful eyes. "One black hair doesn't matter. All of the rest of your face is beautiful."

Reflection

No weapon forged against you will prevail...
(Isaiah 54:17).

Dear God, I know you don't love me based on looks, but it sure feels nice when I do look good. Help me always do my best to reflect the best you've made me to be.

Dress for Success

Seventy-five-year-old Anna is visually challenged. Selecting an outfit to wear each day can be a problem—but sometimes a funny one—like the day she chose a blue-and-white striped blouse and a yellow-and-pink flowered skirt or the time she chose a pair of soft blue jeans when getting ready for church thinking they were her dress pants.

"I'm not exactly a fashion plate," she jokes. "But I do attract attention and that's fun."

Anna said women often walk up to her and ask if they can tuck in a label or clip a loose tag from the back of a T-shirt. "That's actually helpful," said Anna, "but there are times when I'd rather not know what I've done—like the time I wore one red shoe and one blue one. I'd bought two pairs of the same shoe but in different colors. When I grabbed a pair one morning I ended up with different colors. My neighbor Eileen mentioned it to me—meaning well, I'm sure—but all I could think of was how many people had seen me that day in my mismatched shoes."

Anna has come up with a solution with the help of Eileen. They set up Anna's closet with colors and textures in different parts of the closet. Now when she reaches for a pair of blue shoes she knows which shelf to go to. And when she decides to wear a particular dress or pants or skirt, she can feel her way to the section of the closet where they hang.

"I'm still no fashion statement," Anna remarked, "but at least I can be seen in public without being embarrassed. These 'golden years' are not always so golden!"

Reflection

In his great power [God] becomes like
clothing to me; he binds me like the neck of my
garment (Job 30:18, brackets in original).

———————

Dear God, whether I'm in fashion or out, to you I always look good because you made me and you love me. Thank you!

Pretty Feet

Reenie grew up in a family where her mother counted every penny, nickel, and dime…and she expected everyone else to do the same. If apples were 40 cents a pound at Morgan's Market, her mom would drive across town to You-Save, sure to find them for 38 cents a pound, and she was proud to tell the family she'd saved a dime on five pounds of apples. That dime went into an old coffee cup in the pantry till the cup was full. Then her mother added it to her savings account at the bank.

Reenie never had a beauty shop haircut or perm. And a manicure? Why that was practically blasphemy. A healthy scrubbing and filing was good enough, according to Reenie's mother. And foot care? Once a month the kids lined up for toenail clipping. No pretty polish or glitter or hand-painted flowers for them.

As an adult with children of her own, Reenie practiced similar restraints as she made her husband's modest salary stretch like a pair of suspenders in order to keep her family of five in clothes, shoes, and simple-but-good food.

Then one day Reenie looked in the mirror and realized she was still pinching her pennies even though the children had grown and gone off on their own. Her husband had retired from bus driving, and they had a comfortable income.

Reenie took the plunge one day—a plunge into her little savings cup in the pantry just like the one her mother had kept. She pulled out enough money for an eyebrow waxing and a pedicure.

The next month she'd consider a manicure and maybe even a facial. Reenie tingled inside just thinking about these personal treats and how they'd make a difference in the way she felt about herself.

She showed up at the nail shop. When it was her turn she eased her aching feet into the steamy water and sighed as the soapy liquid relaxed her all over. She left that day feeling ten years younger and ten times more beautiful. On the way home she stopped at a shoe store in town and bought herself a pair of open-toed sandals—to display her "new" feet—nails trimmed and painted a lovely shade of pink with a dainty flower on each one. As she drove home Reenie decided the golden years weren't so bad after all. She was no wimp! She had taken an important step for herself, and she had pretty feet to show for it.

Reflection

Immediately he provided her with her
beauty treatments (Esther 2:9).

---

*Lord, how wonderful to pamper my aching feet. They carry
me miles each week, and I want to treat them well. The older
I get the more I appreciate your gift of two good feet.*

Face-Lift

On Monday morning Tonia looked in the mirror. *Oy!* She let out a deep sigh. The wrinkles were taking over her face faster than the snails were ravaging her flower garden. She had to do something and do it quick. She was nearly 70, and time was running out. Pretty soon there wouldn't be enough smooth skin left to push, pull, prod, or pin up!

She sat down at her laptop and spent an hour looking at the many ways she could improve her appearance and lop off a decade or so. There was the usual surgical facelift. And there was nonsurgical microdermabrasion, a peeling of the outer layer of skin, resulting in a smoother, younger look.

She'd also heard about acupuncture treatments for the face. She didn't know much about that procedure but the thought of a bunch of needles poking out of her cheeks and forehead didn't sound appealing.

What to do? Tonia hoped she'd find just the right procedure for her and the money to carry it out. She decided to pray and wait—and see what answer God would bring.

That afternoon she ran a few errands—dropped off clothes at the cleaners, picked up a few groceries, paid her phone and utility bills.

While walking to her car in front of Top Hill Market, Tonia spotted Angie Cranwell, her neighbor's grown daughter.

"Tonia, hi," shouted Angie as she ran up beside her. "How are you? It's been such a long time since we've seen each other. You look wonderful."

Tonia hugged Angie and asked a few questions about the young woman's family, work, and her new home.

Angie was quick to share details. Then she glanced at her watch. "Oops. Gotta run. Have to pick up Robbie from preschool and then meet a painter. We're having the entire house brightened up a bit."

Tonia squeezed Angie's hand and kissed her cheek. "I'll have to stop by when you're finished. I'd love to see what you've done."

Angie smiled. "Absolutely." Then she paused for a moment and leaned in. "Tonia, I must say you look beautiful. I hope I'm half as attractive as you are when I'm your age. Just seeing your smile gives me a lift." With that she turned and dashed to her car.

Tonia stood in the middle of the driveway stunned. *Did I hear Angie correctly? That my smile gave her a lift? What an unexpected compliment!*

Tonia drove home, plopped the groceries onto the kitchen table, and ran into her bedroom. She stood in front of the full-length mirror and surveyed her face once again. She liked what she saw: bright blue eyes that sparkled, even white teeth, a pleasing hairdo with soft, blond highlights, and a smile that had lifted a friend's day.

"Thank you, God," she murmured. "I get it. The best face-lift—and the most affordable—is a smile."

Reflection

The king is enthralled by your beauty; honor him,
for he is your lord (Psalm 45:11).

———————

Dear God, I lift my face in praise to you this day.

Footloose

Sandy stopped at Shoes for Less to buy a pair of white-strapped sandals and a pair of open-toed flats to go with her new pink-and-white capris. She found exactly what she was looking for. In fact she was especially pleased because the flats were the same brand as a pair she'd purchased a year ago—and they were so comfy, great looking, and good for walking too.

Sandy returned home feeling happy and satisfied with her new look. She slipped into the sandals and wiggled her toes up and down. The new pedicure made all the difference. Then she stepped into the open-toed flats. They pinched. She couldn't understand why. The pair she'd slipped on in the store were comfortable. She checked the box. Maybe she'd picked up the wrong size or maybe the clerk put the shoes into the wrong box.

Sandy sighed. This meant another trip to the store. Why couldn't clerks pay attention to their jobs? Those little airhead 20-somethings would rather chat on their cell phones than wait on customers. The more energy she gave to her thoughts the more upset she became. She would tell that young woman a thing or two. Didn't she know how inconvenient it is for senior citizens to have to make two trips to the store in one day? Sandy worked herself into such a state that she feared she'd have an accident while driving. She picked up the shoes and tossed them into the box. Suddenly she noticed something she hadn't seen before. Each shoe had a cardboard lining to help hold the shape of the shoe. She realized she'd been trying to walk around with the cardboard still in place.

It wasn't the clerk's fault...it was hers! A wave of guilt washed over her, and then she sat down and laughed. "These golden years sure ain't for wimps! Dear God, forgive me for being so self-righteous," she prayed.

Reflection

Let us not be like others, who are asleep, but let us
be alert and self-controlled (1 Thessalonians 5:6).

———————

Lord, I sure can spend a lot of time on my high horse. Time to come down and pay attention to what I'm doing.

Take the Cake

Bread and Jam

L ydia woke up early on Monday morning. She stayed in bed a bit longer than usual so she could look again at the cards and notes and letters stacked on her bedside table from her birthday party the previous Saturday night. The number of people who wished her a happy ninetieth nearly matched the number of candles on the cake her granddaughter Mandy had made from scratch—a New York-style cheesecake to commemorate Lydia's city of birth nearly a century before.

She sat up and dangled her legs over the side of the bed, thinking back over her long life. At the same time Lydia felt a bit dismayed. She wasn't sure she deserved all this attention. She'd lived a good clean life and that was that. No need to make a big deal out of it. She got where she'd gotten because of the grace of God, and because she contended for the long life that he promises to those who love and obey him. She didn't see why reaching 90 was any more deserving of a celebration than reaching 10 or 32 or 67.

It was nice, though, to reread the prayers and wishes of her family and friends who had stopped to write. Some had even come by on Sunday afternoon to kiss and hug her in person and enjoy a piece of the cheesecake decorated with fresh flowers from Mandy's garden.

The lemon-mint tea with just a dollop of honey was lovely too. It had been her favorite flavor ever since she could remember.

As for the cheesecake, well it was good of Mandy to take the time to make it. After all she had three young children to take care of. It's not as if she had hours to spare making a fuss over an old lady. But cheesecake just wasn't high on Lydia's enjoyable foods list. She debated about letting Mandy know her feelings on the matter. Since her granddaughter had gone to so much effort, why didn't she go a step further and make a lemon chiffon cake or a double fudge chocolate or a pecan crunch with French vanilla frosting or...

The doorbell stopped her in her thoughts. "Coming," she called as she padded softly to the front door in her new faux fur-lined slippers.

It was Mandy! "Hello, darlin,'" Lydia said, embracing her granddaughter as the women walked into the kitchen. "What brings you by? Whatever it is, I'm glad to see you."

"Just checking up on you, Grammy. You all right? You had a lot of excitement over the weekend." She walked to the counter and touched the cake dish that held the remains of the huge cheesecake she'd made. "I thought you'd have finished this off by now," Mandy joked.

Lydia couldn't lie. But she didn't know how to tell the truth either—given this delicate situation. She hesitated.

"Grammy, is something going on?" Mandy wrinkled her brow.

"I'm afraid you wasted your money and your time on the cheesecake, much as I appreciate all that you did to honor me."

"Grammy, it was my pleasure. Don't you know how much I love and admire you?"

Lydia cleared her throat and braced herself against the counter. "I do indeed. That's why it's hard to admit what I think I should."

"And what is that?"

"Well, dear," Lydia said in the sweetest tone she could muster, "the cake filling is as smooth and tasty as butter itself, but the only way I can eat butter is between two halves of a hot biscuit with strawberry jam on top!"

Mandy laughed so hard Lydia was afraid she'd fall over. "Oh, Grammy, you do take the cake," said Mandy. "Pardon the pun! Thanks for telling me cheesecake isn't your favorite. It's okay."

After a few closing words, the women hugged goodbye and Mandy slipped out the door with a wave.

The next morning the doorbell rang just as Lydia was about to sit down to a cup of lemon-mint tea with a teaspoonful of honey. It was her granddaughter—again!

"Here you go, Grammy," she said, a twinkle in her eye indicating a bit of mischief up her sleeve. She handed Lydia a bag.

Lydia opened it and gasped. Nestled in bakery tissue paper were two golden biscuits, warm from the oven, and a miniature jar of strawberry jam.

"Just a little something to go with your cheesecake butter," she said and then planted a kiss on Lydia's forehead. "Enjoy!" With that she slipped out the door again, and Lydia sat down to enjoy the treat.

Turning 90 definitely had its plus side. She could speak up, be heard, and even better, have her wishes granted!

Reflection
The cheerful heart has a continual feast
(Proverbs 15:15).

———————————

Lord, how nice to be able to speak the truth and have it received in the spirit in which I offer it.

Cake Walk

Molly was known for her cakes. Double-Mint Fudge. Heavenly Lemon. Apricot Angel Food. She'd whip up a cake for her book group, for the Sassy Seniors Club, for a grandchild's birthday party, or for a church potluck. She was known all over Hollow Haven as the "Cake Lady."

Word spread like frosting on a Cinnamon-Spice Ribbon Cake. Soon her cell phone was going off day and night. Invitations poured in as fast as batter into a pan. Would she be a guest on *The Morning Show? The Afternoon Show? The Evening Show? The Weekend Show?*

"Sure."

"Be glad to."

"I'd be delighted."

Before long Molly had covered all the local shows—for 200 miles or more around her little town. Then came an invitation from a show in Los Angeles—a long way from Hollow Haven. The producer and host had seen a write-up about Molly on the Internet. They had a low-budget show broadcast from Los Angeles to San Diego only, so there was no money to fly guests from other states, and they only did in-person studio interviews—no tape recordings accepted. But if she were ever in their vicinity they'd love to feature her on their daytime show *America Cooks*. They did a baking segment on Friday afternoons featuring some of the best pastry chefs west of the Mississippi.

It didn't matter that Molly had never been west of the Mississippi herself. Or that she'd never heard of the show before. Nor did she know the names of any of the big shots they had mentioned. She'd been too busy baking her own creations in her own kitchen for more than 40 years.

Still, it would be a real adventure to go to the West Coast and be on television. Why, all her friends could tune in and see her do her thing on camera in one of those fancy studio kitchens she'd seen on *Regis and Kelly* or on the *Rachael Ray Show*.

Molly checked her savings account. With a little skimping here and there for the next few weeks, maybe she could pull it off. She phoned the producer back and said she could come in June.

Then she called her friend Sadie and coaxed her into coming along. "We'll make a fine time of it," she said. Sadie agreed and their plans took shape. The two friends bought new outfits, and they each got a new pair of shoes and a bag to match.

Three weeks later they arrived at Los Angeles International Airport and took a limo to the studio—show confirmation and cake recipes in hand. When they arrived, a plump woman in a red sweater and purple pants led them into the waiting room. Molly looked around. She didn't see any lights or cameras. And there certainly wasn't any action!

She sat on the edge of her seat wondering if she'd made the worst mistake of her life. What kind of a reception was this for the Cake Lady? Maybe she wasn't as famous as Julia Childs had been, but she was no slouch either. She'd won enough blue ribbons at fairs to decorate an entire wall of her den if she wanted to.

Just then a man with jet-black hair and a wide smile walked in and shook her hand. "I'm Ken Crandall, producer of *America Cooks*. Welcome to our radio show."

"*Radio* show?" Molly surprised herself with the volume of her voice as she stood up.

"Yes. Were you expecting something else?"

"Well, yes. I mean, I thought being a cooking show and all that this was TV."

Ken scratched his head in thought...or was it embarrassment? Molly couldn't tell.

"Far as I know it's always been radio."

Molly pulled out her letter of confirmation and sure enough, plain as the wall behind Mr. Crandall, it said in bold letters: KOOK-AM Radio.

Molly flushed. She'd spent a bundle to get here—airfare, a new outfit, a limo, and she'd talked her friend Sadie into spending some of her savings too. And what about all the people back home hoping she'd bring a tape of this show from Los Angeles to share with them? Well, it was too late for apologies or embarrassment. Here she was in the "City of Angels" on a radio show far from home. She was going to make it work. She smiled and introduced Sadie.

"Shall we get started?" Mr. Crandall stepped aside and motioned the ladies to a small room with a table, a jumble of wires, headphones, microphones, and a pretty woman with blond hair and fake eyelashes. Molly took a seat at the table, and Sadie sat beside her smiling from ear to ear.

Next thing Molly knew, she was talking and laughing and answering questions and sharing recipes with Mrs. Crandall, Mr. Crandall's wife, the host of the show, and with the wonderful callers who phoned in to hear firsthand from the famous Cake Lady who had come to Los Angeles all the way from Hollow Haven—east of the Mississippi.

Reflection

From six calamities he will rescue you; in seven no
harm will befall you (Job 5:19).

———————

*Lord, even when I misunderstand you are here to help me
continue on with good humor and a positive outlook.*

Secret Recipe

Maddy took joy in creating beautiful and delicious birthday cakes for everyone in the family—from her own children to the grands and great-grands. Even close cousins got in on her generosity. She took orders a week in advance of their big day. Specialties included Blueberry Buckle, Mellow Vanilla, Chocolate Harvest, and Cinnamon Apple. And for the health-conscious she'd whip up a carrot or zucchini cake using fresh, garden-grown vegetables and organic flour and sugar.

Everyone looked forward to dessert when Maddy was present. Her cakes were not only tasty, but they were also lovely to look at with flowers or ribbons on top, special lettering, and unique candles. In 40 years of cake baking, she'd never missed an important birthday. Family members and friends asked for her secret recipes, but she guarded them carefully.

One Friday night Maddy's daughter, Cindy, her family, two of Maddy's cousins, and three close friends surprised Maddy at her house for her birthday. Cindy walked in with a Lemon Swirl Cake.

Maddy cried when she saw the lovely creation, complete with 75 candles and fresh daisies on top. "It's beautiful," she said, and wiped her eyes. She took a deep breath. "What's your secret?" she joked, mimicking her daughter who'd asked her the same question for years.

Cindy tapped her lips with a finger. "My lips are sealed. On the other hand, if you tell me your secret, I'll unveil mine."

Maddy and Cindy winked at one another and dropped the subject. The family gathered around the old oak table, which had been in Maddy's family for half a century, and ate the Lemon Swirl Cake with generous scoops of French vanilla ice cream. Then they sang songs around the piano like in the good old days, the ones Maddy so enjoyed talking about.

At the end of the evening Maddy spoke up. "I've been holding on to my secret for a lot of years, but now that I'm getting older, I have fewer years ahead than behind. I want to pass on my birthday cake-baking secret to the next generation." She looked at her three grandchildren and one great-grandchild. "That way you can carry on this tradition when I'm gone."

A hush fell on the room as Maddy disappeared into the kitchen and returned with a brown bag. "Ta da!" she said and whipped out a box of vanilla wafers. "This is it!" she proclaimed.

"Vanilla wafers? What does that have to do with making a perfect cake?" Cindy asked.

Maddy noted the puzzled tone in her daughter's voice. "If a cake sinks or turns out lopsided, and believe me some of mine do on occasion, I take a couple of vanilla wafers, or chocolate wafers if I'm baking a chocolate cake, and slip them under the part of the cake that's sagging. I frost the entire creation, and no one knows the difference. The wafers are so mild, their flavor blends right in. Another secret? Save that section of the cake for the last serving or eat it yourself."

Cindy burst out laughing. "Mother, if you don't beat all. That's it?"

"That's it, honey. Now it's your turn. What's your secret?"

"I came prepared," Cindy admitted. She held up a label from the front of a box of Westbury Lemon Swirl Cake Mix.

"Now that's a secret worth keeping," Maddy said with a twinkle in her eye.

Reflection

We live by faith, not by sight (2 Corinthians 5:7).

———————————

Lord, it's never a secret how much you love or care for me.
You went so far as to give up your life so I could be set free.
That is so awesome!

Playing Games

Who's on First?

"Grams, you have to play. That's what we're here for." Lola looked up from her seat on the bleachers. She had come to the fundraiser to help her grandson Charlie earn money for a trip to a major-league baseball game in Chicago. Fans had paid $10 each to watch a slow-pitch softball game between the junior league players and their grandparents. All proceeds would help pay the team's airfare.

Lola nudged her husband, Russ. "You play, honey. You'll be great—just like you were when we met. Remember?"

Russ rolled his eyes. "No dice, Lola. We both agreed to support Charlie. I wrote the check. You said you'd take a turn at bat. Now keep your promise."

Lola breathed hard and stood up on wobbly legs. She could barely throw a ball, much less hit one. She couldn't see well in the bright sunlight, and if the ball hit her glasses, then what?

She took a deep breath, stepped down from the bench, and took her place in the batter's box.

"Go, Grams, go!" nine-year-old Carla called from her seat.

Lola's daughter Kathy stood up and waved a silk scarf. "You can do it, Mom!"

Lola stepped up to home plate when she heard her name called.

The pitcher lobbed the ball. It seemed to be headed straight for her nose. She swayed a bit and then smacked it with all her might. She looked up as the ball arched over second base. She'd done it—a solid hit! The kid guarding the base and those in the field scrambled but no one could catch it. Lola made it to first, and the grandfather ahead of her slid into second. *Safe!*

Lola wiped her forehead and took her position—ready to move when the next batter took his turn. She was darn proud of herself. If only her mother could see her now. Lola had heard over and over that she had no talent for sports. Well, that might have been true at 10, but at 65 she was a star!

Of course it took more than a little getting ready to come this far. That morning she'd spent at least an hour putting herself together. First she cleaned her glasses and put in her removable dental bridge. Next she tied her hair into a ponytail and shoved it into a baseball cap she'd borrowed from Charlie. Then she pulled on her sweatshirt and baggy pants and stepped into a pair of baseball shoes her niece had loaned her. And finally she wrapped her ankle in an Ace bandage, dabbed a bit of makeup on her cheeks, and added blush and lipstick.

If this doesn't beat all. Life is full of surprises. A broken ankle just before Christmas, my sixty-fifth birthday in February, and now charity baseball in May. What's next? I'm afraid to imagine.

The coach called Lola to the batter's box at the bottom of the eighth. *Whack!* She hit another single and made it to first—out of breath when she arrived, but she got there. Surely that counted for something.

It did. Lola went to bat at the top of the ninth too, and she pounded another ball right over the second baseman's head. That drove two team members home and the victory went to the "old" folks, 3 to 2.

"Congratulations!" called the young coach. "How'd you do it? I'm impressed."

Lola adjusted her glasses and pulled the bill on her cap. "Trifocals, a broken ankle, and a removable dental bridge. Works every time! You oughtta try 'em!"

The young man walked away scratching his head but smiling.

Reflection

He gives strength to the weary and increases the
power of the weak (Isaiah 40:29).

———————

Dear God, when I give my all—whether to play a game or complete a task—you're there cheering me on. Thank you for helping me keep on going...even during these golden years.

Ten Again

Gordy stopped his grandmother at the door. "Nana, don't forget. I'm turning 10 next Saturday. We're having a party in the backyard and you're invited, okay?"

Nana Joan ruffled Gordy's hair. "I wouldn't miss it. See you at two. Your mom already gave me a heads-up. Now if you'll excuse me," she said, "I have some gift shopping to do."

Gordy waved goodbye, and Joan walked to her car.

When she arrived at Gordy's house the following Saturday Joan was dressed for action. She was as fit as a farmer and proud of it. Everyone admired her tennis game. She had been undefeated for the past three years in women's singles. Even the 40-year-olds were amazed at her powerful serve and her quick movements on the court.

Joan walked out to the backyard where five 10-year-old boys were roughhousing and shouting. It was a wild scene, but no harm was being done. The boys appeared to be having fun so Joan was not about to stand in their way. In fact she decided to join them. More games would start right after refreshments.

Gordy's dad laid out a platter of sliced pizza and soft drinks and told the boys to grab plates and dig in. "And don't forget to pick up a napkin!" called Gordy's mother through the kitchen window.

Joan filled up on the goodies and enjoyed every bite. She gave herself permission to indulge on her grandson's birthday. Afterward Gordy's dad suggested a game of Freeze Tag. Joan clapped her hands at the announcement. That had been one of her favorite games as a child. She had to play it again for old times' sake.

"Yea, Nana!" Gordy called. "Look, guys! Isn't my grandma cool?" That's all Joan needed to spur her on.

"Mom, take it easy," her daughter warned. "I don't want any broken bones on my watch. And you're not as young as you used to be."

Joan waved her off. She wasn't going to take orders from a person she'd given birth to. "Respect your elders!" she shouted back and broke out laughing.

Minutes later Joan was rushing around the yard, jumping over logs, rounding trees, and then dropping to the ground when the leader called "Freeze." Suddenly it was Joan's turn to yell. She rolled over and yelped, pulling her right leg to her chest. She moaned in pain and couldn't get up without help.

Her son-in-law carried Joan to his car and rushed her to Urgent Care. She found out quickly that she had pulled her hamstring. The pain was excruciating. She wouldn't be playing tag of any kind for a long time and no tennis for at least a year while she went through intense physical therapy.

The moral of her story in her own words? "When someone says, 'You're not as young as you used to be,' believe it. Or, more to the point, grandkids' birthday parties ain't for wimps!"

Reflection

Though he stumble, he will not fall, for the Lord
upholds him with his hand (Psalm 37:24).

Lord, thank you for holding me up—especially when I call for help!

Blue Cheese or Swiss?

Lois walked up to the front door of her friend Martha's house willing to do her good deed for the day, but she was also determined not to get sucked in again to this woman's chronic complaints.

For Martha there was only one word that described her life: *difficult*. Nothing seemed to go her way.

She resisted the aging process.

She didn't much care for her neighbors.

She was allergic to chocolate.

Her knees weren't working.

She couldn't see as well as she used to.

Her son didn't call her often enough.

Her sister forgot her birthday nine years out of ten.

The pastor of her church never visited.

Even the flowers in her garden seemed against her. They died before they bloomed.

Martha welcomed Lois but made sure her friend realized what a sacrifice it was for her to have company on such a cloudy day. Lois sat patiently as Martha unloaded her woes.

"It sounds as if you could use some prayer," Lois finally cut in. "I think you're in a rut that only God can get you out of."

"I have prayed," Martha said. "Heaven knows I've pleaded with the Lord, but he appears to be busy with other folks."

Lois drew a breath and leaned forward as Martha laid out a plate of cheese and crackers to share. Lois nibbled on a Wheat Crisp as Martha continued her litany of complaints and resisted prayer—the one help she needed most.

Thirty minutes later Lois put up a hand to stop Martha from saying another word. She'd had it with this ornery woman who only thought of herself. She talked on and on without reaching for a snack or drawing a breath! Lois held out a cracker and a wedge of cheese. "Martha, would you like some cheese with that *whine?*"

Reflection

No discipline seems pleasant at the time...later on, however, it produces a harvest of righteousness and peace (Hebrews 12:11).

———————

Lord, help me be a good friend. You never asked me to allow complainers to strip me of my peace. May I know when to listen and when to speak up.

Map Search

Barry and Ginger packed their car, thanked their friends Phyllis and Greg once again for their overnight hospitality, and backed out of the driveway. Phyllis waved and turned to go in when suddenly a horn sounded. She looked around, and Barry was flagging her from the open window on the driver's side.

"Help me get out of here, will you? After the fiasco we had arriving, I don't want to rely on my memory. I need a map or some very clear directions."

Greg stepped forward. He pointed this way and that and spieled off a list of left and right turns that made Barry dizzy.

"Slow down!" Barry stated. "Give me the simplest route, even if it takes us a few extra minutes."

Greg cleared his throat and started over. "Turn right at Monroe—right there at the corner, right again on Tipton, left on Arch and take that directly to Highway 202 going north or south…"

Ginger leaned across the steering wheel. "We're going north to Santa Luisa."

Phyllis couldn't stand it another minute. Greg was all wet with directions—as usual. She piped up. "Greg, Arch Street doesn't go to the freeway. It ends at Highway 96. That highway goes to the freeway, but it's too far south. They want to go north. I'll handle this."

She tugged Greg away from the window and stepped into his place. "Turn right at Monroe, right again at Tipton, and then right at Fairway. Take Fairway all the way to the freeway. You'll pass through two lights. Just keep on going, and you'll sail right onto the ramp going north. This'll save you a couple of miles at least, and there are no confusing turns or intersections."

As Phyllis spilled out the directions, Ginger jotted them down. She read them back, and Phyllis gave her a thumbs up. By that point Greg was upset, bordering on angry. He shouted over Phyllis' head. "My way is more direct. She'll get it when I show her the right way later today."

Phyllis refused to be put down in front of their friends. "Greg, stop it. You're making a scene. Arch Street will not take them to the freeway. I'll show *you* later on."

Barry could hardly wait to get going. He waved, gunned the motor, and shot down the street and turned right.

Greg and Phyllis barely spoke the rest of the day. Finally Phyllis couldn't stand it another moment. "Greg, I'm sorry for losing my cool today. I wish I wouldn't let you get to me, but when you give people inaccurate directions and then act as if I'm wrong, it really hurts."

Greg lowered his eyes and then smiled. "I'm sorry too."

That afternoon the couple took Arch Street to Highway 96. Sure enough, Arch ended at that intersection by curving right and taking on a new name—Riverdale Road. If their friends had known that little fact there would have been no confusion, but Greg hadn't provided that detail. And besides, the route was out of their friends' way since they were going north.

Phyllis pointed out the details to Greg. He furrowed his brow and then grudgingly conceded. "Well, if you put it that way, okay, you're right. But I left out just one minor detail. How big a deal is that?"

Phyllis threw up her hands, and then brought them together and prayed for patience.

Reflection

Let us not become weary in doing good, for at
the proper time we will reap a harvest if we
do not give up (Galatians 6:9).

———————

*Dear God, just when I think I have all my coins in a row, I
discover one missing or out of order. Please help me today to
be less strident and more peaceful, even when other people
annoy me.*

Hot Dog!

H omer loves hot dogs and has ever since he was a kid when his grandpa took him to the ballpark. Dogs and chips and soda were as important to the baseball experience as the final score. But Homer is 67 now, and the trim physique of his youth has given way to a bit of a front porch.

Paula, his wife, is very conscious of it. In fact, she admits she spends too much time reminding Homer that he needs to knock off the hot dogs and learn to love seafood and veggies. He waves her off, avoiding her nutritional advice. He figures he got this far in life eating his way, so why change now.

One Saturday afternoon Paula had a yen for the specialty at Logan's Deli on Main Street. "Homer, would you run out to Logan's and pick up a couple of Greek wraps? We could have a little picnic in the backyard like old times. I'll fix some lemonade and whip up a batch of the vanilla wafers you like so much."

Homer pulled on his chin and furrowed his brow. "I'm in favor of the picnic and the cookies, but a Greek wrap? No way. My idea of a wrap is a soft little bun around a juicy hot hog. I'll get a wrap for you and a dog for me. How's that?"

"No way!" Paula put her hands on her hips. "You know how I feel about fatty hot dogs."

Homer put his hands on his hips. "And you know how *I* feel about them." He noticed the frustration in his wife's eyes. He decided to make a deal. "Tell you what. If I find a parking place in front of Logan's, I get to have a hot dog. If I have to park down the block, I'll go along with you and get a wrap."

Paula let out a deep breath and laughed. "You're on! There hasn't been a free space in front of Logan's on a Saturday for two decades. Can't imagine there being one today, but hey, if there is, you deserve to win."

Homer took off whistling. He just knew today was the day he'd have his hard-won hot dog. He pulled onto Main Street a little later, parked, walked into Logan's, ordered the wrap and hot dog, paid for them, and sailed home, feeling pretty good about himself. He'd won—and he had done so honestly. He'd parked in front, just as he bargained for.

He walked into the kitchen. Paula was waiting, lemonade ready, cookies cooling on the counter.

"Well?" she queried.

Homer noticed the self-satisfied glint in her eye. "Well what? Here's your wrap and here's my dog."

Paula's blue eyes deepened. "You found a parking place in front of Logan's on a Saturday? Amazing! How'd you do that?"

Homer sank into his chair, stifling a laugh. He held onto his hot dog with a death grip. "I had to drive around the block six times first, but I did get one."

Reflection

Truthful lips endure forever, but a lying tongue
lasts only a moment (Proverbs 12:19).

Lord, I admit it. I'm stubborn and shortsighted sometimes. I know what you're teaching me, but I resist because I want my own way, whether eating a hot dog, watching a TV show I should avoid, or winning an argument. Please help me to stop making deals and willingly submit to your voice.

Travels

Some Croc

"The Amazon? Let me get this straight. You want to take a trip to the Amazon—as in the jungle in South America. Is that right?" Ruby's 40-year-old daughter, Angela, planted her hands on her hips and grilled her 63-year-old mother as though she were a teenager asking to ignore curfew.

Ruby crossed her arms and took a stand. "Yes, as in South America. Yes, as in jungle."

"Whatever for? I'll buy you a *National Geographic* DVD. How's that? Mother, there are crocodiles in the jungle. They eat people. What are you thinking?"

Ruby pulled a brochure out of a drawer in the den. "I'm thinking of going, that's what I'm thinking. Mercy and I have been talking about this since we were kids. It's something I've always wanted to do, and if I don't go now it might be too late. I'm not getting any younger, you know."

Angela paced the hardwood floor. "That's my point, Mom. You're not only not getting any younger, you're already elderly. It's not safe. I won't hear of it."

Ruby wagged her finger at her daughter. "I'm your mother! You can't boss me around." She laughed and then waved the brochure. "Besides, it's a done deal. I'm leaving in two weeks."

Angela sighed, rolled her eyes, and laughed. "I might have known. You've been a risk-taker all your life. I can't change you now." She hugged her mother and off she went.

Ruby lay in bed that night thinking about the excitement and adventure that was ahead. The next two weeks disappeared in a blur of packing, settling things at home, and saying goodbye to family and friends.

The plane trip was smooth and uneventful. Ruby breathed in relief as they landed. The following evening, Armando, the native guide, led Ruby and Mercy and six others in small wooden boats up the Amazon River.

"I will show you Caiman. Small crocodiles. Come out at night. Look close and you see them." Armando pointed to the spotlights he would use to find the eyes of these reptiles as they lay on the riverbank.

An hour into the ride Armando spotted a croc, jumped out of the boat, grabbed it, and carried it in his boat back to the campsite for further viewing.

"How about a photo of you holding the crocodile?" Mercy suggested to Ruby when they were settled around the campfire. "Then you'll have something to bring Angela that will show her a thing or two about her mom."

The women giggled but inside Ruby wasn't so sure. It was one thing to look at crocs on the beach from the safety of the boat, but to hold one was another matter. Maybe she should quit while she was ahead. Still, this was her chance to prove herself. She decided not to sit on the sidelines like some little old lady who was afraid of her shadow. Ruby gulped and sat down on a log. Armando picked up the three-foot reptile and laid it in her open arms. Ruby's heart pounded, and she felt a rush of moisture gather in her armpits. She was scared stiff, but she couldn't back out now. She had traveled thousands of miles to make this dream come true, and she'd likely never have another chance. Mercy snapped a photo.

The croc was as silent and still as a stone. "Put him down nice and easy," Armando instructed, ready to pounce if the croc had a sudden burst of enthusiasm.

Ruby placed the scaly Caiman on the sand. The little fellow slid into the water while Ruby slumped against the side of the log and breathed deeply. What a story she'd have for Angela...and a photo too!

Reflection

Be strong and courageous. Do not be terrified; do
not be discouraged, for the LORD your God will be
with you wherever you go (Joshua 1:9).

Lord, thanks for keeping me safe when I step into a new adventure and for giving me the courage to take risks that stretch and strengthen me.

Easy Does It

Nate couldn't wait to retire. He had it all planned. His wife, Wilma, was all too aware of the itinerary: sleep, TV, sleep some more, then more TV. But Wilma was ready to cut loose. They'd been house-bound for years raising a large family, caring for aging in-laws, and taking in every stray cat and dog that came to their door. After 49 years she wanted to dance and travel and take art lessons and walk barefoot on the beach. And she wanted to do all of this with Nate. After all, wasn't that what marriage was all about? Doing things together, especially after their responsibilities had lessened?

Wilma's friends agreed with her. They were eager to kick up their heels too. Wilma's neighbor Glynnis offered her dime's worth: "Just sign him up for dance lessons or book a cruise or fix a picnic for a day at the beach but don't tell Nate till that day. Or at least till it's too late to get your money back—for a trip, I mean."

That sounded like a great idea to Wilma. Why put up with Nate's resistance? She was sure he'd have fun once he got to wherever she planned for them to go. Wilma was suddenly jazzed. She made a list of all the things they could do together and then browsed the Internet for details. After a couple of hours surfing the Net she had a good idea of prices, places, and package deals.

One night while playing cards with Glynnis and her husband, Jim, Wilma announced with a tremor in her voice the next step in her new plan. She cleared her throat and said her piece. "I have some exciting news!" she declared, looking from one person to another.

All heads turned in her direction, especially Nate's.

"What's this?" he asked. "You haven't said a word to me. What's going on?"

"I've looked into a cruise...on the Mississippi River. The price is right, the dates are perfect, and now that you've retired there's not a thing to keep us from having a little fun as well as a nice rest."

Nate sat forward, arms locked across his chest. "I have a different plan. I'm not doing anything. And I won't even start that till noon." He looked around the table and then at Wilma.

She could tell he was looking for approval so she nodded in agreement. "What a good idea," she said with a satisfied smile. "And you can start doin' nothin' at noon the first day of the cruise."

Reflection

My people will live in peaceful dwelling
places, in secure homes, in undisturbed
places of rest (Isaiah 32:18).

———————————

Lord, please help me avoid my tendency to be lazy. I want to participate in life, and yet when it comes to getting off the couch and actually doing something I back out. Strengthen me today so I will live my life to the fullest!

Not My Club

One thing for sure, Patsy was not going to be one of those old ladies with gray corkscrew curls all over her head, plump arms that jiggled when she reached for a glass of water, and a belly that spilled over her waistline—or what was left of it. She couldn't stop the aging process, but she could control how she looked while going through it. She kept her weight in line, walked for an hour every day, attended a dance workout two days a week, and on a very good day she wasn't above climbing part way up a tree with her five-year-old grandson. No senior club for Patsy. She was going to be "forever young"…at least in her mind.

Patsy lived her life with this attitude and commitment. She carried it with her when she and her husband signed up for a cruise in the Bahamas one week in July. She bought a new batch of summer clothes, including cut-offs, flip-flops, a big straw hat with a blue-and-white ribbon, and a jeans jacket with the words MAJOR BABE embroidered on the back. A daring move, but one she enjoyed. If people looked her way in dismay, well, at least they looked. That couldn't be all bad, could it?

At 72 she was a major babe in every way—at least to her way of thinking. She still sang solos in the church choir, headed up a committee on civic fiscal responsibility in her community, and taught a Bible study to a group of 30-something women. She was also a respected member of a group of retired businesswomen.

The day she and Herb boarded the ship, however, she thought she'd crumble. It seemed everywhere she looked there were gray heads—and many of the women had the corkscrew curls she detested—some gray and some blond and some brown—as if they were trying to fool someone. What club was this, anyway?

She and Herb were planning to cut a rug when the music came on that night. They always cleared the floor when they danced, and she was determined to walk the deck every day to keep her figure in check. Four laps equaled a mile. So 12 laps would give her three miles—taking up an hour—the amount of time she walked at home.

The first night in their cabin Patsy poured out her concern to Herb. "I think I made a big mistake. We're with a bunch of old people, and I don't like it. I was hoping there'd be some people like us. All I'm seeing are crow's feet, turkey necks, bald spots, gray curls, and floppy arms. We're in the wrong club."

Herb sidled up to Patsy and put his arm around her shoulder. He steered her to the closest mirror. "Take a good hard look at us, sweetheart. This *is* our club."

Patsy let out a long sigh and then a hearty chuckle. Herb was right. He had a turkey neck. She had crow's feet, and the flesh on her arms—though slender—jiggled at least a little when she reached for a bath towel. And her hair, wavy and attractively cut, was gray going on snow-white.

They dressed, walked to the dining room, and sat at a table of people new to them—yet familiar at the same time. They were all in this together—upstanding members of the Golden Years Club.

Reflection

They will still bear fruit in old age;
they will stay fresh and green (Psalm 92:14).

———————

Lord, this is my club. I'm a senior now, and I need to give myself to where I am, not where I wish I were.

All in a Name

Fred and Inez were having the time of their lives touring Italy. They had signed up with a well-known tour company, eager to have all their needs met: no baggage to lug, no tips to worry about, no money to exchange, no worries about a foreign language. They could sit back, relax, and enjoy whatever the tour guide planned.

As they walked around Lucca, visited the Vatican in Rome, and took a gondola ride in Venice, Inez wished their church friends Helen and Rick were with them. "They would appreciate every detail," she shared with Fred one night as they crawled into bed and read the agenda for the following day.

Fred looked perplexed. "Helen? Rick? I'm not tracking with you," he said. "You know how I am with names. Give me some clues."

Inez threw up her hands. This "forgettable name" game was getting on her nerves. And it was b-o-r-i-n-g! What would it take to get her husband over the hump? He claimed he remembered faces more than names...and that faces were the important things.

Inez didn't agree. "People love the sound of their own names," she argued. "You could do better if you tried. As soon as you meet someone, create a little 'hook' to help you remember, such as Redheaded Rosie or Shirttail Sam." That game had backfired too.

Inez looked at Fred across the ship cabin and went through the usual hints when it came to Helen and Rick. "The couple we've played cards with. She has blond hair, and he has green eyes and talks in a Southern drawl. Remember? They have a German short-haired pointer and..."

Fred's blank stare showed her he was no closer than when she started.

Inez pulled a few more clues out of her mind, but they didn't work either. She was tired of this routine and just plain exhausted after such a long day. She kissed her husband goodnight, turned off the light, sank into her pillow, and closed her eyes.

Suddenly Fred was shaking her vigorously. Inez sat up, switched on the light, and looked at the clock. Two o'clock in the morning! "Fred, it's the middle of the night. Are you okay?"

Fred scratched his head. "Yes, I'm fine, but I'm wide awake. I just got who Helen and Rick are. We've played cards with them, remember? She has blond hair, and he has green eyes...and I believe he has a Southern drawl. Oh and they have a German shorthaired pointer."

Inez yawned and stretched. "Good. That's a start. Now let's get back to sleep. We can talk about it in the morning."

"Talk about what? I can't remember why you mentioned them in the first place. How about a few hints?"

Inez picked up her pillow and bopped Fred on the head. "Here's a big hint," she said, swallowing a smile. "If I don't get some rest, you'll be sleeping on the deck by yourself tomorrow night."

Fred patted her arm and dropped back on his pillow. "'Night, honey. What's your name again?"

Reflection

Even when I am old and gray,
do not forsake me, O God (Psalm 71:18).

———————————

Lord, I am so thankful you know my name and I know yours. In fact, I can call you by many names—Wonderful Counselor, Comforter, Holy Spirit, Father—and you answer to them all.

You're in Charge

Hank watched his wife, Lorna, push herself into the narrow seat on the tour bus, tucking her ample hips between the armrest next to the aisle and the one between them. She rummaged through her handbag, huffing and puffing and mumbling something he couldn't understand.

"Hank, do you have our room key?" Lorna asked as she poked his arm.

He pulled it back and snarled, "No. You said you'd put it in *your* purse because you didn't trust me to keep track of it." There! He'd made his point.

Hank settled back and looked out the window. He took a deep breath. It was a lovely day. A soft breeze wafted over the trees, and the flowers around the edge of the walkway to the bus held their pretty little heads high. It was going to be a good day, and Hank was glad to be alive.

"Well, I don't have it. You must have done something with it. Look for yourself. It's not in the little zipper section where I always put it," Lorna growled.

Hank clasped his hands and twiddled his thumbs. He looked straight ahead. "Now, Lorna, don't go making a scene. I do not have the key. We'll get another one at the hotel desk when we return. No problem."

"What about my audio set? You were going to get it from the guide in the lobby."

"I got mine. You said you'd get yours. You didn't trust me to remember." He pulled his audio player from his pocket and showed it to her.

Lorna blew out a big breath. Hank could tell she was about to make a huge scene right here in front of a busload of people.

"Here, take mine. I don't need it. I'll stand close to the guide."

Lorna pulled a tissue from her purse and blew her nose so loudly the people across the aisle glared in her direction. "You're something, you know that? I ask you to handle two simple things—a key card and my audio player, and you forget both. What's to become of us? I can't do everything."

The bus lurched forward. Lorna's purse slid off her lap onto the floor.

"Sorry, folks," the driver announced. "Just a pesky rut in the road."

Hank leaned down to scoop up the contents of Lorna's purse. He picked up a lipstick, a hairbrush, a plastic card (their room key card), headphones, a package of breath mints...and what was this? A small black audio player with Lorna's tour number on it.

He couldn't hold back a self-satisfied grin. "Looking for these?" he asked, holding the items in front of Lorna.

Her face turned from pink to red. Little beads of perspiration dotted her nose and cheeks. "Now, I remember!" she cooed. "I tossed them in the zipper section on the outside of my bag and forgot to close it up. I was in a hurry and...and I'm sorry, Hank."

"All's forgiven," he said and took her hand in his. He reached into his pocket for his earphones and audio player. Then *he* broke out in a sweat.

"By the way, dear, do you have an extra set of earphones by chance? I must've dropped mine or left them in the room."

Reflection

Woe to those who are wise in their own eyes and
clever in their own sight (Isaiah 5:21).

———————————

*Lord, the minute I feel self-righteous show me how human I
am. Thank you...I think.*

Smooth Sailing

Lindon propped up his pillow and pulled a book off the shelf over his night table. His wife leafed through the cruise brochure. Rosemary turned to him. "What if I get seasick? I'm not sure I'm up for seven days on a boat."

Her husband rolled his eyes. "Ship, darling! *Ship*...not boat."

Rosemary leaned over. "I'm not up for seven days on a *ship* either."

Lindon put down the book. "Think about it, honey. We won't have to cook, make our beds, do our laundry, or drive our car. We'll be totally pampered. We can snooze, read, stroll, shop, watch a movie—you name it! As the song goes, it'll be 'just you and me, baby.'"

"Well..." Rosemary thought for a moment. "All right I'll try it. But if I get sick, I'm going straight home. Oh, but I can't do that, can I? We'll be at sea. I'll be stuck in a boat and sick to my stomach in the middle of nowhere."

Lindon flinched. He wondered what he was getting into. Why had he sent for the brochure in the first place? He and his wife could just as easily stay home, watch TV as they did most nights, and order out so they wouldn't have to cook. They could leave their bed unmade and their car in the garage any time. The thought depressed him. He was tired of the same ol' same ol'. Clearly it was time for a much-needed change, for an adventure on the high seas! Rosemary wasn't excited about it, but she hadn't ruled it out either. He'd decided to risk it.

Lindon booked the cruise and three months later he and his wife walked up the gangway and onto the ship bound for Alaska. For an entire week they ate fabulous food, visited interesting ports, including Juno and Ketchikan, enjoyed live stage shows each evening in the ship's theater, and even danced in the Sky High Room.

Rosemary admitted she was reluctant to see their vacation at sea come to an end. It had been smooth sailing for seven days. On the final evening, however, the ship suddenly swayed. Guests strolling the walkways reached for the handrails to avoid losing their balance.

Rosemary panicked. "Lindon, just what I feared. I'm going to be sick!"

The captain announced over the intercom system that one of the stabilizers had malfunctioned, and they'd have to cruise with only one in place. It was not dangerous, just inconvenient.

The ship made it to port, and the disembarkation process began. Soon Rosemary and Lindon were on their way home. Rosemary had managed to hold on to her stomach contents despite the final rough hours.

As they fell into their own bed that night, she turned to her hubby and hugged him tightly. "Thanks for a wonderful week!"

Lindon sat up. "Really? I thought you'd want to bop me after what happened last night."

"I got to thinking about my attitude," she admitted. "You were trying to bless me and I resisted. When I finally surrendered, I had a fabulous time. The little upset on the way home is minor compared to all the good things we experienced all week." Rosemary fluffed her pillow and snuggled up to her husband. "I believe God used this experience to teach me something. When we go with the flow and trust him as the Captain of our ship, it's smooth sailing even when we hit the rough spots, even when we think we're going to fall overboard. He always guides us back to shore."

Lindon didn't know what to say. The tears in his throat choked out any words.

"'Night, honey," whispered Rosemary. "By the way, I'd like to cruise the North Atlantic next time. I'll call for a brochure tomorrow—if you're up for it!"

Reflection

Others went out on the sea in ships; they were mer-
chants on the mighty waters. They saw the works
of the LORD, his wonderful deeds in the deep
(Psalm 107:23-24).

———————

Lord, you teach me your ways even when I resist. Help me appreciate the opportunities you offer and learn from any obstacles.

Bedroll Blues

Sam, recently a widower, decided to go on a cruise to help take his mind off the loss of his wife a few months before. He missed her terribly. A friend suggested the Danube River in Europe so he could spend time in some of the Old World cities such as Vienna and Budapest—places he and Florence had always wanted to visit. It sounded good to Sam so he called a travel agent and signed up for a Viking Cruise.

The first night onboard proved to be a tricky proposition. The bed in his cabin was made up "European-style," according to a neighboring shipmate. Each bed had a pillow and a hefty comforter folded vertically in thirds. No extra blanket was provided and no spread like his bed at home in the States—the kind he'd been used to ever since he could remember.

Sam decided to be good-natured about the change, since he couldn't undo it. When in Vienna do as the Viennese!

That night after a satisfying dinner and a cappuccino, he retired to his cabin and got ready for a restful sleep. He showered, stepped into his new blue-and-yellow striped pajamas and slipped into bed—sort of. He put the pillow on the floor so he could sit at the top of the bed and slide into the bedroll. But the more he maneuvered his body, the more twisted and tangled he became. He couldn't seem to get the hang of getting into the middle of the three-fold without it falling apart. First one side would open and then the other...or his feet would stick out at the bottom and get chilled.

He wondered how any European could get a decent night's sleep if this is what he had to put up with every night. Finally Sam settled for sleeping on top of the quilt with a coat pulled over his body. He wore a pair of socks to keep his feet warm. By morning he was exhausted. It had been a night of tossing and turning, losing the coat, and nearly rolling off the bed. He was anxious about how he was going to sleep for the rest of the trip. He approached the front desk after breakfast and told the clerk his dilemma. "Any suggestions for an American who isn't used to this European bedroll you all use?"

The clerk looked at Sam, smiled politely, and made a reasonable suggestion. "Sir, tonight when you go to bed, unfold the comforter and lay it over you in any way that is comfortable for you. It is plenty long enough to hang over the foot of the bed so your feet will be covered and stay warm."

Sam felt his face heat up.

The clerk smiled again. "Is there anything else I can do for you, sir?"

Sam slunk away from the counter. "Can't think of anything at the moment. Thanks." He turned and waved with a limp hand. "I'm heading back to my cabin now...for a good day's sleep."

Reflection

When you lie down, your sleep
will be sweet (Proverbs 3:24).

Dear God, when I get confused or discombobulated, you're here for me, making sure I can stand on my feet when necessary...or lie down and get some sleep!

Tall
Tales

I've Got a Secret

Minnie liked to gossip. She knew she shouldn't tell on other people, but it was so much fun to see the glint of interest or shock in the eyes of those she spoke with. She rationalized her guilt away by telling herself she didn't spread rumors. She only told what was true. For example, Gilda had been coloring her hair since she was 19, poor thing. Lennie had bragged he'd written a book but in truth he'd only written one small paragraph included in the last chapter of a manual at work. And her neighbor Belva watched soap operas even though she was a highly educated woman.

Minnie would never pass really private information such as Mrs. Mendoza down the street running up a huge bill at Linton's Department Store that left her husband in a financial bind or Elizabeth eating cat tuna once when her Social Security money ran out before the end of the month, which it wouldn't have if she hadn't bought a $100 blue silk blouse. She wanted to catch the attention of her neighbor Henry in time for him to invite her to the senior dance on Valentine's Day.

No sir. Such things were much too personal to share with others. The only reason she knew about them was by chance. She liked to ask questions, and she loved to eavesdrop. She just couldn't help it.

Like her mother before her, she was a curious sort. She was interested in people and their unique challenges and problems.

Minnie went along this way for a good many years. She knew things others never knew, and she enjoyed having this place of prominence—even if such prominence was in her mind only.

A day of reckoning came, however. Minnie had a secret she wanted to guard with all her might. She'd lost her head and heart to a man she met on a cruise to Alaska. He was a gentleman of 75 years and was handsome with a white mustache to match his white hair. He shared her faith in God. Harold was a widower with a grown daughter and a faithful cat whom he named Lenore, after his deceased wife.

They met for coffee, then for dinner, then for a bus trip to the Garfield Museum, and then for a home-cooked meal at Minnie's house and a DVD about Queen Elizabeth. The day after the "meeting" at home, Minnie noticed someone bouncing up her walkway. Neighborly neighbor that Belva was, sure enough she inquired about the attractive man with a white mustache who had arrived early and stayed late.

Minnie felt her cheeks flame and her heart pound. She wasn't ready to announce her feelings to the world, and certainly not to her nosy neighbor—who really ought to mind her own business. A simple dinner and a movie with a gentleman friend was nothing to gossip about.

The thought barely crossed Minnie's mind when she realized she was really speaking to herself. She ought to mind her own business. And now she had some important business to mind—her growing feelings for dear Harold.

"I'm keeping company with a nice man," she told Belva in a matter-of-fact way. "And I'd appreciate it if you wouldn't pass this on. We're still getting acquainted. It's my secret for now."

Belva held a hand to her mouth and chuckled. "No problem. Didn't you know that seniors are the safest people in the world to share your secrets with?"

Minnie frowned. No, she didn't know that.

"They can't remember the secrets two minutes after they've heard them," Belva said. "So your secret...now how does that go again? Your secret is safe with me!"

Reflection

The words of a gossip are like choice morsels; they go down to a man's inmost parts (Proverbs 18:8).

Lord, this is funny. When I was a kid I couldn't keep a secret, but it wasn't because I couldn't remember it. Now I'm in my second childhood, and I can keep a secret till my dying day...if I can remember it.

Say Cheese

Lucy was a party animal—even at age 75. She loved good food, festive decorations, sparkling beverages, and dressy clothes. She'd drop everything at just the hint of a shindig. So when her best friend, Thelma, decided to throw a party for herself on her eightieth birthday, Lucy was the first to say yes to the invitation.

The night of the affair Lucy was giddy with delight. She danced with Thomas and James, two of the single men in her group of friends. She helped pour the fruit punch at the table by the door. That way she could see who was coming and going and get dibs on the people she wanted to sit and talk with.

The highlight of the evening was the professional photographer, Benny, who looked as if he were fresh out of high school with his smooth skin, full head of black hair with just the right amount of gel, and cool blue jeans with a striped shirt hanging over his belt line.

When he called people to line up for their photos with Thelma, Lucy abandoned the punch bowl and headed to the next room. She straightened her skirt, checked her lipstick in a nearby window, and pulled out a mirror and mini-brush to touch up her curls. Then she ran her tongue over her teeth to be sure there were no threads of strawberry from the punch clinging to one of them. She was smile-ready and excited about having the opportunity to be on-camera with her best friend on such a special occasion.

"Glad-hand Fritz" walked up behind her and clapped her on the back. "Ready to show those pearly whites?" he teased.

Lucy felt her face flush. He must have caught her checking her teeth. "As a matter of fact I am," she replied, and turned her back to him. He was one of the bachelors in their group who was an annoyance to nearly everyone—especially the ladies...and particularly Lucy.

"Next!" Benny called.

Lucy took her place behind the white line beside Thelma.

"Big smile now," Benny cooed. "And your name?"

"Lucy."

"Beautiful teeth, Lucy."

Lucy was about to say thank you when Fritz leaned forward and shouted, "And they're all hers!" He laughed out loud, apparently proud of his quip. So proud he didn't know when to shut up. "Not sure about the hair, but the pearly whites are genuine, right, Luce?"

"Why, Fritz!" she retorted, stretching out her words with fake sincerity. "I bet you wish I could say the same thing about yours."

Lucy smiled, Benny clicked, and the photo shoot was history. So was Fritz.

Reflection

He is my shield...my stronghold (Psalm 18:2).

———————————

Lord, what fun to have the last word. It's not always the right thing to do, but sometimes it is. Please help me know when it is and when it isn't.

A Turn of Phrase

Eighty-five-year-old Garth strolled slowly with the help of a cane through the San Diego Museum of History with his 55-year-old son, Glen. The men were both history buffs and especially enjoyed reliving early-American history together through reading, watching DVDs, and talking about various aspects of the Revolutionary War.

They came to a display window featuring the Redcoats. Garth's memory wasn't what it used to be, so he needed a bit of help remembering who was who and what the men stood for. Glen patiently explained to his father that the British Redcoats fought to keep control of the American colonies, and the white stripes across the front of their uniforms signified the aim of their fire. They held their guns over one shoulder and followed through over the white line on their jackets.

Garth nodded as Glen continued with more details than his aging mind could handle. He nodded in agreement from time to time so his son wouldn't think him rude or uninterested. He hung on to the term Redcoats so he could continue the conversation when they were driving home.

After an hour or so of browsing the sites and reading the many placards, Garth suggested they stop at the nearby cafeteria and order lunch, his treat.

"Fine by me, Dad," Glen replied.

Off the pair went in search of a sandwich and a cold drink. As they sat across from one another at a small table in the corner of the outdoor deck, a loud buzzing suddenly sounded close to their ears. Glen flicked his hand at a large insect circling his father's head.

"Watch it, Dad," he shouted. "That critter is after you."

Garth looked up and saw a flicker of yellow and black. He ducked and batted his hand. Exasperated, he shouted, "Get away you nasty yellow coat!"

Reflection

He gives strength to the weary and increases the
power of the weak (Isaiah 40:29).

———————————

Lord, this tickles my funny bone...maybe because it's so familiar. I can slip on a word here and there like a skater on ice. But with your help I pick myself up and keep going.

Murder, He Said

D rew loved watching movie reruns on TV or DVDs of old murder
mysteries. He noted the titles in a notebook, and as he watched
them he put the date and a check mark next to the title so he wouldn't
watch or rent it again too soon. Now that he was 78 and counting,
he noted that he'd watched a total of 453 films in the murder-mystery
genre over the last four decades, give or take a few.

Dial M for Murder, Diagnosis Murder, and *Manhattan Murder
Mystery* were among his favorites, but as he aged he wasn't as quick
to recall the plot lines. He depended on the notebook to determine
whether or not he'd seen a particular movie lately.

One Saturday afternoon Drew drove to Drive-Thru Flicks to pick
up a few DVDs to pass the time while his wife, Eva, was away for the
weekend babysitting their two granddaughters in a nearby town. He
paced the aisles looking for a film he hadn't seen before. He scratched
his head, wondering what to choose. Some titles *looked* familiar,
but when he read the plot summaries on the back they didn't *sound*
familiar. He felt like kicking himself for leaving his trusty notebook
at home.

He chose a couple of flicks, paid for them, and drove off. *Wouldn't
hurt to repeat one or two if that turned out to be the case,* he con-
soled himself. Later on Drew settled into his recliner in front of the

new big-screen TV while balancing on his lap a bowl of popcorn drizzled with real butter and salt—something Eva would never have tolerated if she were home.

About an hour into the film the phone startled him. He hit the pause button on the remote and picked up the cordless receiver, which he'd placed on the side table next to his chair.

"Drew here," he said.

"Eva here," his wife teased.

Drew could hear the smile in her voice, and it warmed his heart. He missed her. But then he felt guilty when he looked at the empty popcorn bowl and the pot he hadn't yet cleaned and put away.

"Checking in," Eva reported. "The girls and I are calling to see how you're doing."

"Just fine," he said. "Munching popcorn and watching *Diagnosis Murder*. I'm about to find out 'who done it.'"

"But you've seen that movie at least a half dozen times. Remember when…"

"Don't tell me," he scolded. "I want to be surprised."

"How can you be surprised?" Eva sounded skeptical.

Drew bounced back with a chuckle in his voice. "I'm finding there's an advantage to memory fading with time. Even if I saw it before, it's a new movie every time 'cause I don't remember the plot."

Reflection

There is a time for everything, and a season for
every activity under heaven (Ecclesiastes 3:1).

———————

Lord, there are some advantages to the golden years after all!

A Close Call

Bruce and Tim pulled out two of the chairs that faced the breath-taking view of Pike's Peak from the huge picture window on the east side of the clubhouse. They had arrived early for the monthly meeting of the Rocky Mountain High Old Timers Club in Colorado Springs.

Most of the members were men in their 70s and 80s—retired professionals and businessmen who gathered for breakfast, conversation, and relaxation. They loved telling stories of the old days and recalling times when they were young, vibrant, and important people of the community. They also traded a few comments about men who had irked them or situations that just weren't fair. Some hadn't vented their feelings in years, and this seemed to be a safe environment for doing so, especially with other men who would understand what they'd been through.

Failing health in one form or another plagued every member of the club. All the men were practically deaf, one was blind, and others had an assortment of ailments ranging from an aching hip to a stiff neck.

As the men sipped coffee and plowed through the scrambled eggs and fried potatoes, the conversation turned to one of Tim's longtime competitors in the automobile business. Bennett had been an out-standing businessman and community leader.

Tim poked the air with his fork. "Did you know his son Ronald went to Yale with my son?"

Bruce cleared his throat and put in a few facts of his own. "Bennett was a good man. Close to his family too. Beautiful wife, I remember that."

The men chuckled. They may be hard of hearing, but they still had eyes for pretty women.

Tim leaned forward. "One thing I liked about ol' Ben...and Ronald too for that matter—they were loyal friends and had good business sense. You couldn't pull a fast one on them, and they were never vicious if someone tried."

Just then a 30-something young man walked over and excused himself for interrupting. "Couldn't help but overhear your conversation," he said, and reached out to shake a few hands. "Bennett, the man you're talking about, why he was my grandfather and Ronald was my dad. Both gone now, as you may know. It's nice to hear you talk so well of them both."

He pointed to his mother and brother still seated at a table nearby. "We didn't intend to listen in," the brother remarked, but we couldn't help but hearing our father's and grandfather's names being mentioned.

They chatted for a few more minutes and then said their good-byes.

As they left the room, Tim pulled out a handkerchief and mopped his brow. He turned to his fellow members and smiled. "Good thing we weren't gossiping," he admitted.

Reflection

But I tell you that men will have to give account on
the day of judgment for every careless word they
have spoken (Matthew 12:36).

———————————

*Lord, you guard my tongue and put caring words in my heart
and on my lips. Thank you.*

Seeing Things

Doris opened the front door and walked into the hallway. She could hardly believe her eyes—her *new* eyes, that is. She had just returned from cataract surgery, and she could see clearly now after years of declining eyesight.

Before she left for the surgeon's office, she'd been sure of three things:

» She had a few laugh lines around her eyes.

» She had a bit of gray hair.

» Her kitchen floor was clean because she'd mopped it herself the day before.

Her friend Lyddie had told her the surgery would be a snap. The procedure would last fewer than 15 minutes. She'd be on her way home in less than an hour. But that wasn't her experience. Quite the opposite, in fact. Doris called Lyddie to explain. "The surgery must have taken a toll on me physically," she said, standing in front of the mirror, "because now that I'm home I'm sure of three things:

» I have a lot of laugh lines—not just a few.

» I have scads of gray hair—not just a bit.

» My kitchen floor has dirty spots everywhere. Who's been messing with it?"

The women had a good laugh. Doris was happy with her new view on the world, but not so happy about her view of herself and her kitchen floor. Lyddie suggested three ways to remedy the situation:

» Use makeup more often.

» Make an appointment to dye her hair.

» Hire a cleaning crew.

"Then let's go to a movie and out for dinner," Lyddie proposed. Doris was quick to reply, "You're on!"

Reflection

When I awake, I will be satisfied with seeing
your likeness (Psalm 17:15).

―――――――――

Dear God, thank you for the gift of sight—and for a second chance for new sight when my tired old eyes need some help. May I always clearly see you and your will for me.

Time's a Flyin'

Card Party

June picked up the mail and brought it into the house. She leafed through it, tossing the junk and piling the rest on the kitchen table. The phone rang before she had time to sort the mail into piles for her husband, Marty, her son, Max, and herself.

Marty walked in looking for lunch. He glanced at the mail and noticed an official looking envelope for Max. The return address said Selective Service. Marty remembered then that Max had complied with the law when he turned 18 by registering with this federal agency that recruits untrained men and people with professional health-care skills to help during a national crisis when Congress and the president so direct.

He smiled as he anticipated the letter of enrollment with Max's name on it. Marty took delight in passing the envelope to his son with great fanfare. "Ta da!" He snapped the letter in front of Max when the family gathered for lunch and then announced the change in his son's status.

June reached for the stack of mail and pulled out another envelope—this one for Marty and it too appeared "official." She leaned over her soup and whispered something in Max's ear. Max stood up and delivered the envelope and its contents to his father.

"Ta da!" he mimicked.

"What's this?" Marty unfolded the letter—an invitation to join AARP (American Association of Retired People) and a temporary card till he paid his dues.

"Happy fiftieth birthday, Dad!" Max congratulated. "Looks like we're both in for some changes. I'm growing up, and you're growing old."

Marty put up his dukes and Max matched them. They both laughed, and then turned to their soup that was getting cold.

June covered her mouth to keep from laughing out loud.

Reflection

The glory of young men is their strength, gray hair
the splendor of the old (Proverbs 20:29).

———————

Dear God, it's great to have a little fun with others as I age. I watch my kids grow up, and they watch me grow old. May I keep my eyes on you regardless of my age.

Empty Nest

Nancy and her mother, Janet, sipped tea on the patio of Nancy's home in Pismo Beach, California, on a Saturday in early October. As they drained their cups and nibbled on the last butterhorn cookies, Nancy stood up. "Well, Mom, it's time to go to the airport. Margo will meet you at the gate in New York so you don't have anything to worry about. You're going to have a wonderful visit. I just know it."

Nancy tucked a 20-dollar bill into her Mom's hand and hugged her again. "Buy yourself a treat at the airport on me." Suddenly tears came and she could hardly see to open the door and walk out to the car. She reached into her pocket for a tissue and wiped her eyes. "Mom, what's going on with me? I'm happy for you, but I'm sure going to miss you. We've been together for so long."

Janet settled into the passenger seat in the van and sighed. "It has been a long time. When did I move in? I think it was 1985."

Nancy squeezed her mother's arm as she backed out of the driveway. "I couldn't have raised Jeff and Ellen alone. I'm so grateful you agreed to help me."

"And you helped me, honey. Remember how lost I felt after your father died? Now it's time for Margo and me to be a team. She needs me after her surgery. I think I'll stay for a few months…maybe even through spring. We'll see how it goes."

Nancy pulled into traffic at the light and turned on a Beegie Adair CD. The soft jazz sounds soothed her heavy heart. It had been quite a year. Jeff had been married in May. Ellen had received her master's degree in June and moved to Phoenix to start a new job as a counselor. And now her mother and best friend was moving across the country to live with Nancy's sister for a time.

"I don't know if I'll be able to stand the silence and all the clean rooms," Nancy joked. "I'm suddenly feeling so alone…almost lost. I haven't felt this way since Jim died, and that was nearly 20 years ago."

"Now you know how I felt when you left home. What people say about the 'empty nest' thing is true, isn't it?"

"I suppose so." Nancy smiled and rolled her eyes. "Mom, I just had a funny thought. I left you with an empty nest when I moved out of your house, and now you're leaving me with an empty nest as you move out of mine."

Janet pointed at her daughter and chuckled. "It's payback time, honey. What goes 'round comes 'round."

Nancy nudged her mom with an elbow, and the two smiled as they drove to the airport.

Reflection

I will pour out my Spirit on your offspring, and my
blessing on your descendants (Isaiah 44:3).

---

*Lord, how good to share time with my adult children. They
fly out of the nest so quickly. When they come back for a visit
it lifts my spirit. The old saying is so true: All I have to give
as a parent are roots and wings.*

Taking Turns

Robert put down the newspaper and caught the phone on the first ring. "Robert here."

"Howdy, Rob. It's Milton."

"Milton who?"

"Milton from Possum Trot."

"Hmmm."

"You don't remember me, do you?"

"Can't say I do. I haven't lived there for years. What's our connection?"

"Your bicycle."

"I don't own a bike. Haven't had one of my own since I was ten years old."

"I know. That's the one I'm talking about."

Robert was about to hang up. This man wasn't making sense.

"I looked you up in the Los Angeles phone directory on the Internet. Got me a computer this year. My kids hooked me up to the twenty-first century."

"And?" Robert's pulse elevated. He was irritated.

"I just wanted to check in after all these years. We went to grade school together. Remember Miss Bertie Mae? She taught us in fourth grade—the year you got your Schwinn bicycle with the shiny handlebars."

Robert scratched his head. He barely remembered the bike his father had worked so hard to get him. And here was a stranger who recalled the manufacturer and the color.

"I s'pose you're wonderin' why I called."

"As a matter of fact I am."

"To thank you for letting me ride your bike. I was thinking about it the other day and thought that was a darned nice thing you did for me. I never had a bike, but I felt like I did because you shared yours with me. It means a lot, even after all these years."

Robert felt tears well up in his eyes.

"Well, that's what I called about. I'll let you go now. Nice talkin' to you. And if you ever come back to Possum Trot, drop on by."

In an instant Milton was gone. He didn't even leave his phone number so Robert could call back.

Robert smiled to himself. *Guess I can look you up on the Internet. As you said, Milton, this is the twenty-first century. We can rekindle our friendship—and maybe even plan a bike ride!*

Reflection

Let us not love with words or tongue but
with actions and in truth (1 John 3:18).

Lord, how little I know about how my actions influence and inspire others. Help me share something of myself today that will brighten someone else's day, even if it's just a smile, a nod, a word, or a phone call.

Cheers!

Cora appeared to be in the final chapter of her life. She was 91 and weak from a bout of pneumonia. She barely ate anything anymore. Her daughter Gina called hospice to make her mom's last days comfortable and secure. Three women took turns tending to Cora's physical and emotional needs over the following two weeks. They kept her clean, hydrated, and offered meals or snacks when she was awake and lucid. But Cora wasn't interested in food. She waved her hand over the trays and looked away. Not even a bite of peach pie with vanilla ice cream, her favorite dessert, enticed her. She was not hungry and that was that.

One afternoon as Cora napped soundly in the other room, the hospice workers and Gina took a break for a glass of lemonade. Suddenly a loud screeching poured down the hall from the other end of the house.

Gina and the two women raced into Cora's room expecting to find her on the floor or collapsed in bed from a heart attack or stroke. Instead Cora was sitting up, a doll-sized woman in the midst of a pile of fluffy white pillows.

"I'm thirsty!" she said and smiled as if nothing unusual had occurred.

Gina reached for her mother's hand. "Are you in pain?"

"No. I'm thirsty."

Gina raised her tone. "I was worried about you. Are you aware that your scream nearly scared us to death?"

"No. Are you aware that not getting a drink when I ask for it is nearly killing me?" Cora sank back into the cloud of pillows. "Gina's trying to do me in," she moaned, reaching in the direction of the caregivers. "She won't give me a drink when I ask. That's grounds for elder abuse, don't you think?" Cora smiled and rolled her eyes.

Gina nearly fainted. How could her mother say such a thing? She had taken care of her for five years, putting her own life on hold to do it. And now this? She felt betrayed and humiliated in front of the volunteers.

Gina started to explain. "Every day I offer my mother juice and water, but most of the time she refuses. I have to coax her to take even a mouthful. I don't understand why she's talking this way." Gina swiped at the tears that brimmed her eyes.

Cora pushed herself up with her fists and leaned back on her fragile elbows.

"I'm not talking about watery juice," she said, looking first at one nurse and then another. "I'm talking about a good, stiff drink!"

The women broke up laughing.

It appeared Cora would be around for a while yet. With a sense of humor like hers, and an audience to enjoy it, she wouldn't be in a hurry to crash the pearly gates. Gina went to the kitchen and returned with the straight stuff—unfiltered, organic apple juice.

Reflection

Shout for joy to the LORD,
all the earth (Psalm 100:1).

Dear God, I hope I can keep my sense of humor till my last days. It's good to laugh and smile and bring a bit of joy to others too. May I never lose my ability to do that.

Changes and Choices

Roses Are Red

Roger woke up on Monday morning, rolled over to the side of the bed, and sat up. "This is it! No more TV. No more chatting over the fence with Fred. I've got to do something more with my life."

Roger leafed through a catalog he'd placed on his nightstand. It listed upcoming classes for the spring semester at Logan Community College for adults. He'd always wanted to see his byline in a magazine or on a book cover, but he hadn't done anything to merit it. He liked to talk about goals, but he didn't care much for reaching them. It meant more work than he was willing to invest.

But now that he'd turned 68 and some of his friends were dropping like leaves from a tree in autumn, he decided it was time to grab hold of something and actually see it through. He pulled on his sweats and sneakers, poured himself a cup of instant coffee, and popped a slice of three-seed bread in the toaster. Minutes later he sat down at the computer and pulled up the college's website to enroll in a class on writing for publication. There were many selections to choose from, but writing a story is what interested him most. He knew he had plenty of material to draw on from his own life, so how hard could it be?

Roger filled in the enrollment form, put an X next to the class he wanted, entered his credit card number, and clicked submit. He was set. No turning back now.

The following Monday night Roger showed up at the school and felt really good about himself. Maybe he was one of the oldest dudes on campus, but at least he was willing to learn. That was more than he could say about some of his buddies who had nothing better to do than talk about golf and politics and their aches and pains. He walked into the assigned classroom, opened his notebook, and pulled out a pen, ready to take notes on how to write a novel.

"Welcome to Poetry 101," said the young teacher, a Miss Pritchard. "We'll be studying some of the great poets over the next several weeks, and you'll also have a chance to write a poem of your own by the end of the session."

Roger froze in his chair. Clearly he was in the wrong class. When he checked with the registrar's office at the break, he received word that indeed this was the class he had signed up for and the novel writing course was already filled.

He decided he must have checked the wrong box on the enrollment page. He also determined he wasn't going to back out. He'd set a goal to become a novelist, but it seemed his subconscious was prodding him to be a poet.

Roger returned to class and settled in to the lecture. By the end of the night he liked what he'd heard and was feeling optimistic about what lay ahead. Later that evening as he drifted off to sleep some words came together in his mind.

> Roses are red.
> Violets are blue.
> I'm a great poet.
> I just don't know it...yet!

Reflection

There is surely a future hope for you, and your
hope will not be cut off (Proverbs 23:18).

---

*Lord, like the psalmist, I write my own words of love and
praise to you for all you've done in and through me. I want
to praise you!*

What?

Sally and Debra, ages 53 and 57 respectively, bought an aerobics studio. They'd been looking for something to do now that their children were grown and the grandkids were in junior high. It was about time they started taking up their own lives. The women wanted to feel useful again, to be needed, and to get back in shape. It simply wasn't okay with Sally to have to suck in her belly every time she zipped her jeans. And Debra was determined to give up her hobby—baking pies from scratch. Tart boysenberry with real whipped cream and a sprinkle of cinnamon and caramel-covered pecans was her downfall. She'd pulled Sally into the pie abyss with her, and the two decided they had to do something. Stretching and bending and sliding across the floor to loud music seemed just right. And they'd be doing it with other women—their new clients—so there'd be no going back to their old habits. Then maybe they could afford a slice of pie or two once in a great while, and it wouldn't make that much of a difference on their figures.

After the first year in business, they both looked at each other. Did they want to continue teaching aerobics? Were they achieving their goals? They decided they were, sort of. Sally could zip up her jeans more easily now, and Debra had definitely cut back on pie baking. But were they fulfilled? Was it enough to bounce across the floor, squat, bend, lunge, and do the grapevine day after day? Was there more to life?

"I know," Sally offered one day as she bounded up the steps to the aerobic center, "let's donate blood. The Red Cross has announced a critical need for blood donors. We could go down to the blood bank after class."

"Good idea," Debra agreed. "I've never done that before. It's time I offered."

Later that day the two women drove to the blood bank and were impressed at how many people in their age range were there to donate. They were feeling quite noble as they joined the line of other gray heads. After a preliminary check-in and check-up, they were both turned down! Sally learned that her blood pressure was too high. She'd need to visit a physician first—to see if she had high blood pressure, which might require medication to manage it. Until it was under control, she couldn't be a donor. Debra was even more surprised to be turned down. She'd gotten a tiny butterfly tattoo on her right arm two weeks before "just for fun," as she put it. She discovered that day that anyone with a tattoo cannot donate blood for one year after the procedure.

The women left the blood bank feeling discouraged and rejected—even if for good causes. Debra took a deep breath and held her head high. "There's only one thing to do when you're pushing 60, forgetting things you used to recall easily, and getting turned down by the American Red Cross."

"What's that?" Sally asked, eager to find out the secret.

"Eat pie!" Debra exclaimed and then giggled like a high school girl. "And I know just where to get two slices of boysenberry with real whipped cream and a sprinkle of cinnamon and caramel-covered pecans."

Sally licked her lips and smiled. "I bet you do. Come on, sister, lead the way!"

Reflection

Humble yourselves, therefore,
under God's mighty hand, that he may lift you
up in due time (1 Peter 5:6).

———————————

Lord, thank you that I can laugh at myself when things don't go the way I want them to...or as I expect them to. The important thing is my attitude. May I always hold the light of your love in my thoughts, words, and deeds.

Eat Your Oats

Roland volunteered at the Seascape Nursing Home. He felt it was the least he could do. The old folks needed a helping hand, and he was willing to lend one—or both. He enjoyed reading stories, serving meals, doing magic tricks, and playing the piano, anything to relieve the residents' boredom. He loved making life a bit brighter for these men and women who were more than 75 years old and confined to the facility for one reason or other.

Roland never counted himself as part of this group. He was 82, skinny as a tree branch, and straight as a stick. He walked five miles a day and was proud of it. His hair was thinning, and his muscle tone wasn't as sound as it used to be, but for a man his age he was a pretty fair specimen, if he did say so himself.

One Wednesday morning after breakfast in the common dining room, Roland walked in and played the piano for the oldsters. Afterward he took a seat in the audience and spent a while talking to the men and women.

Suddenly an elderly gentleman with a long beard and bent shoulders stood up and shouted to no one in particular, "Let's sing happy birthday to Roland. It's your birthday, ain't it?"

Roland stood and felt his face turn warm. "Not today. You must have me confused with someone else."

A woman with dyed red hair and pink polished fingernails pulled on Roland's shirtsleeve. "Don't be shy. You're old just like we are."

Roland was suddenly hot under the collar and wet under his arms. In fact he was more than hot and wet. He was mad and more than a little embarrassed. It was not his birthday, and even if it were, he wouldn't admit it here. Everyone in this place was really old. He was simply elderly.

Just then the recreation director walked in. "What's all this commotion about?" Mr. Peters asked. "Are you having fun or is someone in trouble?"

"Having fun," answered the bearded man.

The redhead poked Roland in the belly. "Making trouble," she squeaked. "It's his birthday. We want to sing, and he won't let us."

Mr. Peters wrinkled his brow. "Why not, Roland?"

"It's not my birthday, that's why!"

"I see. Well, apparently there's been some mistake. When is your birthday?"

"Next Tuesday."

"Well that's only a few days away. Suppose we sing now in case you're not with us that day."

Roland put up his hands in protest. He knew the routine, and he didn't like it one bit.

Mr. Peters sat down at the piano and plunked out the happy birthday song. Those who could sing chimed in. Roland gritted his teeth through the song and managed a shallow "thank you" at the end. He sat down.

"How many candles on your cake this year?" asked Mr. Peters, as though he were speaking to a five year old.

"Too many," Roland replied.

"How old are you?" Mr. Peters seemed really curious now.

Roland exploded. He couldn't believe his own reaction. "None of your beeswax." He remembered his father saying that whenever someone asked him a question he didn't want to answer.

Mr. Peters remained implacable. He looked around the room.

"Tell me your age, and I'll give you another bowl of oatmeal," he promised with a smile.

That did it. "Ask me again and I'll turn the bowl over on your head!"

Reflection

Pride goes before destruction, a haughty
spirit before a fall (Proverbs 16:18).

————————

Dear God, I know I can be shy—and sometimes testy—about revealing my age. I wonder why. What difference does a number make? All that matters is that I honor you with the years I have.

Seeing Double

Larry visited his mother at a care facility in Miami, Florida, while passing through on business. She'd been having trouble remembering the names of family and friends, and Larry was sad thinking about the changes in his dear mom. He and his wife had made a point of coming to Miami on his mother's birthday and at Christmas each year for the past three years. And he'd never pass up an opportunity to see her when he was in the area.

He walked into her room on the first floor next to the nurses' station, and there sat his mother. She was 87 now and looking pretty frail, but she still had a sparkle in her gray-blue eyes and her moon-white hair clung to her head in soft curls. She'd always had the most beautiful hair and dainty soft hands.

"Hi, Mom. It's me, Larry. I'm in Miami on business so I decided to come by and see how you're doing." Larry leaned over the wheelchair and kissed her cheek.

"Doin' fine. Just fine. And how are you, young man?"

"Really good. Ann's doing okay too, and Matt and his family send their love. Those grandkids are growing up fast. I have some pictures to show you."

Larry pulled out his wallet and turned to some 3 x 5 photos. He handed his mother the collection to look at.

"Handsome family," she said and handed them back. "Did you tell me your name?"

Larry's stomach clenched. This was the moment he'd feared. His mother didn't seem to know her own son.

"Larry, Mom. My name's Larry. I'm your firstborn, remember?" He pointed to the picture of himself with his wife, Ann, and their son, Matt.

"Where'd you say you live?"

"I didn't say because I figured you knew. We live in Deerfield, Illinois, where you raised me."

"Deerfield did you say?"

"Yes, Deerfield."

Larry's mother's face lit up.

"I have a son in Deerfield. I wonder if you know him."

"Mom, that's me. I'm your son Larry from Deerfield." He felt his pulse jump.

"I'll be," his mother said, looking off in the distance. "My son's name is Larry too, and he lives in Deerfield. That makes two of you. How interesting. Well, thanks for stopping by and when you get back, if you see my son, tell him his mother's been looking for him. It's time to come home. And tell him I love him."

Larry wiped the tears that puddled in his eyes. Then he bent down and kissed his mother's white head and stroked her soft hands. "'Bye for now. When I see Larry I'll certainly tell him you love him."

Reflection

How gracious he will be when you cry for help
(Isaiah 30:19).

Dear God, I have my own problems with aging, but when I see the challenges my parents face, it really gets to me. May I lean on you for courage and strength as we help them together.

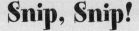

Snip, Snip!

One day Margaret's daughter Ruth called. "Mom, we're having our annual family photo on Saturday at Nobel Park. We all hope you're up for it. Mick and I will pick you up at one o'clock sharp. If you need help dressing or getting ready, let me know and I'll come early. And one more thing. We'll be having a picnic afterward, so bring your appetite. By the way, Will and Jordan will be there with their girlfriends. It's looking serious between Will and Lynn. I can't wait till you meet Lynn."

"Tsk tsk." Margaret was known to "tst tsk" whenever her two grandsons brought new girlfriends around. She wished they'd each pick one, settle down, get married, and give her some great-grandchildren before it was too late. At age 82 she figured she was at heaven's gate.

She agreed to the photo shoot and said she could manage on her own quite nicely. No help needed—at least not yet.

The following Saturday Ruth and Mick met Margaret at her front door. The entire family met at the park. Within an hour the professional photographer was done. Margaret held up her hand. "I'd like a few with my camera," she announced.

Ruth stepped forward. "But Mom, we can get you copies of the ones we just had taken."

"I'd like my own," Margaret asserted. "If you don't mind."

"All right. But I don't see the point." Ruth was clearly agitated with her mother's insistence.

"Get back into formation," Ruth called to everyone. "One more photo for Mom with her camera."

Adults, children, and teens murmured among themselves and gathered reluctantly. Margaret took over. She lined up each person in the order she preferred.

Will wrinkled his brow. Jordan grabbed Amy's hand and pulled her close to him in the second row.

"Lynn and Amy, you move to the ends—one on each side," shouted Margaret, waving her hands and pointing to the spots where she wanted the girlfriends to stand.

Ruth pulled her mother aside. "What's this all about? You're creating a lot of confusion."

Margaret leaned in and whispered to her daughter. "I put the girlfriends on the end so if it doesn't work out between them and the boys—and it probably won't—I'll take the photo and snip, snip."

Reflection

Do not be anxious about anything
(Philippians 4:6).

———————

Lord, this is funny—more so because I can relate to it. I see girlfriends and boyfriends coming and going in young peoples' lives, and I want to hold up a sign that says: Caution! Commitment ahead! But I must step aside and allow them to lead their own lives, covering them with my love and prayers.

Wishful Thinking

The doorbell rang and Josh hobbled to answer it. "We're here!" Greta said, smiling as she reached out to hug her patient. He ushered her into his living room and two other women, Miriam and Lucinda, followed, each one carrying a little kit.

"Miriam will get your bath going. Lucinda will warm up your meal, and I'll turn down your bed and prepare for your leg massage. We're going to get you moving like you used to," Greta asserted as she led the way to the bedroom.

Josh plopped into a chair and sighed. It had come to this. He'd be 84 next May, and he could barely do a thing for himself with his bum legs. Maybe he'd tuckered 'em out by too many years walking golf courses. *I should've taken my brother's advice and ridden in a cart. Oh well. Too late now.* This is the way life turned out. He needed help, and he had to buck up and take it—and be grateful too.

Within minutes he was slurping a bowl of hot tomato bisque soup and chomping on a couple of whole-wheat crackers laden with ham and cheese with a blob of mustard on each one. After supper Miriam helped him into the bathtub and left him for a few minutes to soak in the warm suds. Then she ran a wet cloth over his arms and legs and face. She handed him the cloth and said before turning away, "You wash your you-know-what."

He chuckled, took care of business, and then held on to the railing as Miriam helped him out of the tub and wrapped a warm towel around his body.

Next Greta turned down the quilt on his bed, and Josh lowered himself into its comforting heft. Greta uncovered one leg at a time and massaged it with strong, capable hands. He thought for a second he'd died and gone to heaven, it felt so good. The ache lessened and the throbbing ceased—at least for the moment.

Greta finished her work, tucked the covers under Josh's chin, and planted a sweet goodnight kiss on his wrinkled forehead. The three ladies gathered around his bed and whispered a prayer for good sleep.

Lucinda turned out the light and the women slipped quietly from the room. Greta poked her head in one last time. "Anything else you'd like before we leave?"

Josh sighed. He scratched his balding head and then his eyes sprang to life. He gave a big laugh and announced, "I'd like to be 30 again!"

Reflection

He will renew your life and sustain you in
your old age (Ruth 4:15).

———————————————

Dear God, this is a double-sided predicament. I enjoy being cared for when I need it, but I also wish I were young enough to take care of myself. I choose to be grateful. Thank you for meeting all my needs.

Just Desserts

Ninety-year-old Marvin loved sweets—no getting around that. Chocolate mousse, caramel pecan turtle cheesecake, apple streusel, triple berry cream pie, and any kind of candy or ice cream. The list was endless. "If it's sweet, it's neat!" according to Marvin.

Marvin's doctor didn't share his patient's passion. He was more concerned with Marvin's general health—and his heart and cholesterol, in particular. During his last checkup Marvin half-listened to Dr. Brown's suggestions about curbing the sweets, substituting the high-calorie and high-fat desserts for low-cal, no-fat gelatin treats, or, better yet, fresh fruit.

"Doc, lo-cal, no-fat, no fun, no thanks!"

"Marvin, my job is to help you live a long and healthy life."

"Doc, congratulations. You've achieved your goal," Marvin replied. "I'm 90!" With that Marvin walked out of the office and met his friend Harry for a triple latte with real whipped cream and a slice of double-chocolate fudge at Minerva's Bakery.

Marvin enjoyed telling Harry about the conversation in his physician's office. Harry brightened and leaned forward. Marvin could tell he was about to be lectured. It was something Harry loved to do—tell other people how to live their lives—though he rarely told himself the same thing.

"Marvin, I really think you should give more thought to Dr. Brown's advice. He's been looking out for you for the last 30 years. You owe him that much, don't you think?" Harry sat back and crossed his arms. "I'll support you. We'll give up these decadent desserts and go on a fresh fruit binge. It's summer so it'll be easy with all the berries and melons in season. What do you say? Is it a deal?"

Marvin slammed his fist on the table. His coffee cup jumped. "No deal!" he declared. "Why should I change what's working for me? I love sweets. Enough said. When in doubt, don't change desserts, change doctors."

Reflection

Teach the older men to be temperate…
self-controlled, and sound (Titus 2:2).

———————

Lord, it's tough to be disciplined. I linger over the dessert tray, loiter at the ice cream counter, pace back and forth in the bakery. I'm always tempted to eat what looks and tastes good. Help me enjoy the natural, good foods you have provided and focus on living, not eating.

Wonder Wear

When Liz's husband, Myron, retired, Liz decided they each needed to do their own laundry. It wasn't fair that she carry the entire load, especially now that Myron had so much free time. In fact, she'd like it if he offered to take over the laundry completely...but he didn't.

She had to teach him what to do, but she felt it was worth the hassle. Then she'd be free to do other things with her time. He'd always had more dirty clothes than she did, so it was time for him to discover what it was like to wash and dry and iron. Maybe he wouldn't be so quick to toss a shirt into the dirty clothes after just one wearing and go through bath towels like tissues.

After showing him the ropes, Liz didn't worry about Myron's clothes. But after a couple of weeks went by...and then a month...Liz noticed Myron never seemed to be in the laundry room. She wondered if he was taking his duds to the Laundromat in town and maybe leaving them there for personal service. *Oh well,* she decided, *it isn't my place to question him.* She had relieved herself of the duty and didn't need to go prying into his way of doing things.

Suddenly one day Myron piled a load of dirty clothes—all his—on the folding table in the laundry room. Liz was shocked. She'd never seen so many socks, shorts, and undershirts from one man in her life. Why, the pile rivaled the one she dealt with several days a week when their two sons still lived at home!

Liz eyed the mountain of laundry and was really glad she'd started this new custom or she'd be overwhelmed. She didn't know Myron even owned that much underwear! She went on her way, doing her portion of the housework. A few days later she noticed the pile of clothes was still on the folding table. And then a statement came in the mail from Tipton's Department Store. The total was $100 for men's clothing.

Liz slapped the bill in front of Myron over dinner that evening. "What is this all about?" she asked, a glint in her eye.

"Bought myself some new underwear," he said, a sheepish expression crossing his face. "I ran out so I picked up some more."

"Ran out? You've been buying clothes just to get out of doing laundry? You could've washed what you had and saved us $100!" Liz took a deep breath and let it out slowly.

"I didn't have time. It just seemed easier this way," Myron admitted.

"You didn't have time to do laundry, but you had time to shop?"

Myron chuckled. Liz frowned. Maybe this division of labor was costing her more than she could afford. She decided to come up with a new plan. Then she backed off. If she took over the laundry again that was probably just what Myron was hoping for!

Reflection

Be patient and stand firm (James 5:8).

———————

Dear God, help me be supportive of the people in my life. On the other hand, I don't want to do for others what they are capable of doing for themselves. Please help me find the right balance.

Respect Your Elders

One afternoon Kitty and her mother, Virginia, decided to clean and polish Virginia's silverware in preparation for an estate sale before the elderly woman moved into an assisted-living facility. She was no longer able to live alone. Her forgetfulness was escalating and Kitty, who still worked full-time, was unable to take care of her mother around the clock.

Mother and daughter enjoyed sharing memories of the grandmothers and great-grandmothers who had passed on the treasures now being arranged for the sale. Virginia wanted to give some of the items to her daughters, but there were more than they could use, so a sale seemed the best way to go.

During the course of their conversation, Virginia picked up a set of hand-crocheted doilies, looked at them, and then tossed them on the floor. She was clearly agitated. She blinked and fidgeted with her hands and couldn't express a complete sentence without getting weepy.

Kitty probed a bit, and finally Virginia spilled her feelings about a family member who had given her the doilies as a gift, but then behind her back insulted her good name and had never apologized. She turned to Kitty. "Please don't laugh. This is serious."

"Mother, of course I won't laugh. I can tell this is very important to you. Tell me more."

But Virginia had moved on to something else. "I have a question for you. How old am I, and when was I born?"

"You're 83, Mom. You were born on May 2, 1924—a happy day for all of us who know and love you."

Virginia gasped. "I had no idea I was that old! Am I really 83?"

Kitty nodded and took her hand. "You are—and it's something to be proud of."

Virginia was not so easily placated. "Why couldn't you have just told me I was 25 or 31?" The women laughed but then Virginia grew somber again.

She repeated the name of the relative who had offended. "How *dare* she speak about me that way! Why, I'm an old lady. Somebody needs to tell her to respect her elders."

Reflection

Remember the days of old;
consider the generations long past. Ask your father
and he will tell you, your elders, and they will
explain to you (Deuteronomy 32:7).

Dear God, please give me the grace to accept where I am and to be thankful for it.

Driver's Seat

Sherry volunteered in a soup kitchen at a local church. She loved serving those in need and also enjoyed the friendship she had with the other volunteers, particularly Edna, aged 82, one of the oldest on the team. One Friday morning Sherry and Edna got into a conversation about growing older and how many things one has to give up as the aging process takes over. "I hope I'm as agile as you are when I'm your age," Sherry said, patting Edna on the back. "You're an inspiration."

Edna nodded and smiled. "I know I'll be old—someday," she quipped. "But I still have a few miles to go."

Sherry ladled soup into two bowls and passed them to the men in line. "That's the spirit. These people need you...and our team does too." She paused a moment in thought and then spoke up again. "By the way, Edna, I know it can get pretty dicey out there in traffic. If you'd rather not drive in this busy neighborhood, I'd be glad to pick you up. And if you want to give up driving entirely at your age, Phil and the boys and I would be happy to squire you around—you know, to church, the grocery store, the doctor's office, or wherever you need to go."

The moment the words came out of Sherry's mouth she knew she'd hit a nerve. Edna turned stone-cold and shrugged her shoulders.

"Listen, dearie," she said, "I'll be driving till the day I die, you can be sure of that. I can drive as well as I can walk." With that she turned, took a few steps, and tripped on a storage box behind the counter. Sherry reached out just in time to catch her by the elbow as she hit the floor.

Edna staggered to her feet, brushed herself off, and laughed. "I might need to rethink your offer," she said and gave Sherry a hug.

Reflection

He who trusts in himself is a fool, but he who walks in wisdom is kept safe (Proverbs 28:26).

Dear God, as long as you're in the driver's seat in my life, I have nothing to fear.

Second Chance

Lucille always regretted that she never went to college. There simply wasn't enough money in her family and, besides, she had younger siblings to care for at the time. Now at age 80 she wanted to do something out of the ordinary with what was left of her life. She dreamed of giving young people the chance she never had—a higher education. There were plenty of teens who would gladly seize the opportunity if someone would lend them a hand.

While walking through the mall one day, browsing at one shop after another, Lucille got a bright idea. She'd open a used clothing shop in town, staff it with volunteers, and any profit she made would provide scholarship money for underprivileged college-age students. Maybe her idea would catch on to the point that people would match her funds, thereby doubling the amount available.

Lucille called a meeting of friends from her church and community, shared her vision, and within 60 days she had a small shop rent-free and three volunteers. Used clothing poured in. By the end of the first year, she had enough money put aside to help finance three students for their first year of junior college. Interested young people qualified through a personal interview with Lucille, two references from responsible individuals in the community, and a letter from their pastor or youth leader.

The golden years sure ain't for wimps—and Lucille, more than anyone in her circle, knows how true that is. It's never too late to strike out and do something amazing to help others!

Reflection

Life will be brighter than noonday, and darkness will become like morning. You will be secure, because there is hope; you will look about you and take your rest in safety. You will lie down, with no one to make you afraid, and many will court your favor (Job 11:17-19).

Lord, you are the God of second and third chances—and more. May I keep that in mind as I try new things and step out with faith and confidence when you put a new idea in my mind.

Hip Hop

A tingle raced up Marilyn's spine. There was a dance for seniors at a local church, and she and other guests at Mountain Grove Assisted Living were invited to attend. She hadn't danced in years, but she was certain she'd remember what to do the moment she got out on the floor. Then a fleeting thought punctured her excitement. What if no one asked her to dance? Would it be all right if she did the asking? After all, this was just for fun. Marilyn wasn't planning to court anyone.

She didn't let fear overtake her. She decided to go and that was that. She looked in her closet for her best dress—the light-blue one with a full skirt and puffy sleeves. She could already picture herself whirling across the dance floor.

The following Saturday at six-thirty, a large tour bus arrived at Mountain Grove Assisted Living to take the guests to the church hall. A popular American dinner would be included—hamburgers and hot dogs, potato salad, chips, and for dessert good, old-fashioned root beer floats. Marilyn was sure this evening would be a blast, especially for the seniors she lived with who didn't get out much.

When Marilyn arrived she recognized the church. This had been the place where she had attended several writing conferences in the past. Was this a coincidence? No, there aren't any with God. He always has a purpose. Marilyn was excited to think maybe she'd be the one to write up a little story about the evening for the *Mountain Grove Newsletter.*

When the bus stopped and everyone filed into the church hall, Marilyn was in her glory. The theme was the 1950s, and there was music of that time and the volunteers were dressed in poodle skirts, bobby socks, and saddle shoes. Marilyn remembered a similar outfit she wore when she was in high school. She and others posed for photos in front of a 1952 Chevrolet.

An Elvis Presley impersonator autographed Marilyn's photo and told her she looked pretty in her blue dress with the puffy sleeves. And then he asked her to dance!

"Even though some were in wheelchairs and many used walkers," she later reported for the *Mountain Grove Newsletter,* "we danced the whole night long with handsome men and beautiful women. No one appeared shy! To say the least, we seniors had a great time. In the words of our youth, 'We had a ball'!"

Reflection

Let them praise his name with dancing and
make music to him with tambourine and harp
(Psalm 149:3).

Lord, what a delight to dance in your sight—whether on a dance floor with a partner or in my mind and heart. Your love and joy and peace and protection set my feet a dancin' every moment of the day.

Lost and Found

Keyche, Anyone?

Donna was famous for losing keys. Car keys. House keys. Motor home keys. Safety deposit box keys. The woman simply couldn't hang on to them. Friends and neighbors knew this about her and laughed it off. Her husband and grown children, however, didn't think it was so funny. They carried extra sets with them for that inevitable call when Donna was stranded somewhere unable to go here or there or get into or out of this or that.

One Tuesday afternoon Donna called her neighbor Maureen and invited her and her husband for dinner. "I'm making quiche with fresh zucchini from my garden and the cheese Mom brought back from Holland. I tried it on Hal and he approved, so we can share it with you and Bob."

Maureen accepted. "Thank you. What a treat! See you at six."

Donna spent the afternoon preparing the elegant dish. She also made a fruit salad with fresh strawberries, raspberries, and blueberries. She topped it with whipped cream and chopped nuts.

She'd forgotten to plan a dessert when she'd been at the grocery store so she decided to run back to the market and pick up some chocolate chip cookies and sorbet—a light dessert for after the egg and cheese dish.

Donna grabbed her purse, but when she reached for her car keys they weren't there. She looked everywhere—bathroom countertop, the shelf in the laundry room, the bookcase in the den, beside the TV in the living room. Nada. No. Not there. Or there. Or there.

Donna sank into an easy chair in the den and pouted. She was as fed up with her careless habit as was everyone around her. There was no way she'd call her neighbor Maureen, or her daughter, Jane, or her husband, Hal. No one was sympathetic to her lost-key syndrome anymore. That settled it. No sorbet or cookies. She'd make do with ice cream sundaes with banana slices and butterscotch sauce. She had those items on hand.

That evening as Maureen, Bob, Donna, and Hal ended their meal, Donna excused herself to fix dessert. Maureen offered to help.

"Sure thing. Pull out the ice cream, and I'll slice the bananas."

Maureen opened the freezer and reached for the carton of ice cream as Donna stood beside her at the kitchen counter. "What are these?" her friend exclaimed, laughing as she picked up a set of frozen keys and dangled them in front of Donna's face.

Donna gulped but recovered nicely. "Keyche, of course," she said, laughing, realizing she'd laid them down on the ice-cube shelf as she stocked her freezer after grocery shopping.

Reflection

The Lord is my helper... (Hebrews 13:6).

———————

Dear God, I do the dumbest things sometimes. I keep surprising myself! I wonder if this silly behavior is really mine. But yes, it is. I'm glad I'm not alone, that you are in the trenches with me, especially when I need a ladder to get out.

Here Yesterday, Gone Today

C harles, have you seen my white cotton sun hat?"

"No. Where'd you have it last?"

Such questions were becoming routine in our household. If Charles wasn't asking me the whereabouts of his sunglasses, I was asking him where I put a certain pair of socks or a pillow or now my favorite sun hat. This had never been the case with me before...before I turned 60, that is, but now that I'm pushing 70—and pushing it hard—I'm noticing I'm becoming a bit more distracted. Okay, downright forgetful.

I thought about where I'd last seen the hat. I'd worn it on a walk with a friend one morning. After that Charles and I went grocery shopping and then out for lunch. I remembered having the hat with me in the market and at the restaurant. After that—nothing. A dead end.

The search continued for weeks until I'd exhausted every possible spot in our home and cars. I could only assume I'd laid it down on the bench in the restaurant and gone off without it. I checked with the manager, but he hadn't seen it. So either I didn't leave it there *or* someone took off with it.

C'est la vie. I had to let it go. Twice I came across other white hats in boutiques and shops we visited, but none could compare to the one I misplaced—in style, comfort, or price. I wore an old one I didn't like very much and told myself I'd have to "make do" since I was responsible for the loss.

I did ask the Lord to lead me to my missing hat, if it was within my grasp. And I mentioned that I'd love to take it with me on our next vacation. We were to leave in a week. God heard me and delivered quickly. He knew I was running short on time! I took my suitcase down from the closet shelf a couple of days later so I could begin packing a few things at a time. I opened a zippered section that I rarely use to see what I might fit in that compartment for the upcoming trip. *This is a good spot for a floppy hat or a paperback book,* I thought as I reached inside.

What's this? I had left something behind the last time I used the bag. There it was! My soft, white, floppy hat! I suddenly remembered I'd taken it on my last trip.

I pulled my hat out and hugged it as tightly as I might a long-lost friend. In a way it was exactly that. I was so excited! I put it on immediately and invited my husband to go for a walk with me.

"On one condition," he said with a wrinkled brow.

"And that is?"

"That when we get back you put it in the closet with our other hats—where it belongs—until we pack for our trip. Then you'll know where to find it."

I smooched him good and agreed. Then we went for our stroll—I in my newly found sun hat and he in his favorite bill cap.

Reflection

The Lord is not slow in keeping
his promise (2 Peter 3:9).

———————————

*Dear God, I could open a clothing shop with all the clothes
and accessories I've lost and found and then lost again over
the past few months. I feel like an absent-minded professor!
Help me be more careful and mindful of what I'm doing.*

A Dog's Life

Bert and his dog, "Baby," were the best of friends. Bert uses the word "were" advisedly after what happened a week ago. He went out for his usual Monday night game of Bridge with his three neighborhood cronies. When he came home it was dark and cold—colder than usual for an October night. Bert looked forward to cuddling up on the sofa with Baby. They'd watch a little late-night TV, check on the news, and then turn in for a good, long sleep. Baby needed her rest at age 15 as much as Bert needed his at age 82.

Bert walked in the front door and called for Baby. Usually the dog responded right away with a lick and a tail wag. She wasn't as spry as she had been, but then Bert wasn't too spry either. They had a lot in common as they grew older together.

But this night Baby didn't come running or even walking. She didn't come at all. Bert got scared. He worried he'd find her on her back, dead of a heart attack or some other ailment.

"Here, Baby! Daddy's home, sweetheart. Come on! Time to watch our show, remember?"

Still no sound. Not even a whimper for help.

By that time Bert was whimpering himself. He combed every inch of the house, the closets, under the bed, the corner of the living room, beneath the kitchen and dining room tables. Still no Baby. He was frantic. He threw open the back door to call to his next-door neighbor for help, and there lay Baby, huddled in the cold, tied to the tree where Bert had left her when he went out to put gas in his car.

Suddenly it came back to him. He wanted to make a quick stop, and then hurry home to feed Baby and himself before he left for the Bridge game. But he forgot his plan, and Baby suffered because of it.

He untied Baby's leash, picked up her shivering body, and carried her indoors. He turned on the fire in the gas stove, and the two sat together warming themselves. Then Bert fixed Baby a good meal—including some bits of hot dog, her favorite treat.

The next day Bert went to an office supply store to purchase a pad of sticky notes. He wrote a reminder on two of them—"Bring Baby in before you leave"—and posted them by the front and back doors. Now when Bert goes out without Baby, he is reminded to bring her in before he leaves.

Reflection

I was young and now I am old, yet I have never
seen the righteous forsaken (Psalm 37:25).

Lord, I know you never forsake those who love you, and you don't let go of our pets either. You created them and you care about them. May I always remain attentive to the small creatures of the earth and treat them with lovingkindness.

Closed Case File

Oh those happy golden years! Al was firmly situated in the midst of them. He had just celebrated birthday 79. To hear him tell it, it wasn't exactly a celebration—more like a nod to another year with the hope there'd be a few more, God willing. The day after Al's birthday he went out for coffee and donuts with his pal Gig. The two had been friends since college and lived near one another most of their adult lives. After a good talk and a few laughs, each said goodbye and drove off.

Ten minutes later Al slid out of the driver's seat, slammed the door, and strolled through the front door of his house, still thinking about the fine time he and Gig had enjoyed as they reminisced about the good old days.

Later that day Al offered to pick up some cleaning for his wife. He walked out of the house and realized his car was not in the driveway where he'd left it!

He shouted to Gloria. "Did you move the car?"

"No, I've been here all afternoon." She looked through the front window. No car in sight. She picked up the phone in the den and called the local police. An officer came right over and took notes to file a stolen vehicle report. "We'll get on this right away," he assured the couple.

Al knew things were in good hands so he calmed down, and then walked to his next-door neighbor's house. He was sure Stan would loan him his car for the short run to the cleaner's.

As Al strolled toward the front door, he spotted his Dodge. What was it doing in Stan's driveway? Then it dawned on him. He had pulled into Stan's by mistake. The two driveways were right next to one another, so it was understandable, though he'd never done such a thing in the ten years he'd lived here.

No harm done. Just a silly oversight. He reparked his car and walked into the house to tell Gloria. Before he could utter a word, she handed him the phone. "Officer Benson for you."

Al's heart pounded. "Yes, officer. I understand. Sir, before you continue let's just say the case is closed. In fact, I solved it myself."

"Where was your vehicle?"

"In my neighbor's driveway—where I parked it."

Al detected a snicker on the other end of the line.

"All right, sir. I'll mark your file 'Case Closed.'"

Reflection

In all your ways acknowledge him, and he will
make your paths straight (Proverbs 3:6).

———————

Dear God, this story is too close for comfort. I'd be the kind to drive to the store and then walk home...and later think someone had stolen my car from my garage. Thank you for watching over me—and my antics—day and night. And thank you for coming to my rescue when I need it!

I See, You See

Jan walked into the house from the front yard where she'd been weeding and watering. *Whew!* She was bushed, to say the least. The temperature had risen to 90 degrees, and she was drenched in perspiration. She pulled off her sweaty shirt and shorts and took a quick shower. She got dressed and stretched out on the sofa for a few minutes of rest.

She was just about asleep when she realized she was still wearing her glasses. She removed them quickly and placed them on the table beside the sofa. She awakened an hour or so later and glanced at the clock, but she couldn't see the numbers clearly. She reached for her specs…but they weren't there. *Must have fallen on the floor,* she decided. Jan reached around the end table and under the sofa. No trace of her glasses.

That meant locating her spare pair, but she couldn't remember where she'd put them…somewhere for safekeeping. They were safe all right, perhaps forever!

"Don!" she called to her husband. "I've misplaced my glasses." She raised a hand. "I know what you're going to say: 'Again?' There, I said it for you. But, honey, this is different. I know I put them on the table when I went down for a nap. We're the only ones home so what could have happened?"

Don blinked but kept his commentary to himself. The two searched for the missing glasses for about 30 minutes when Jan noticed her husband's glasses perched on their dresser in the bedroom.

She picked them up. "By the way, hon, if you're looking for your glasses here they are." She handed them over.

Don pulled off the glasses he was wearing. "Then what are these?"

Jan shook her head. "For Pete's sake. They're mine!"

The two had a good laugh. "I have an idea," she said. "Since you're able to see perfectly out of my glasses, we can buy just one pair from now on and save ourselves a couple hundred dollars."

Don didn't take to that idea. He didn't intend to be that thrifty. He returned Jan's glasses to her and donned his own.

Reflection

Do not take advantage of each
other (Leviticus 25:17).

May I see your face, dear Lord, with or without my specs.

Telling the Tooth

Roxie and her husband, Maurice, were part of a Bridge group. They played the card game every Friday night. Once a month they all went out to dinner together. Each couple took a turn choosing the restaurant. In May, it was Roxie and Maurice's turn.

"I vote for Barney's Barbecue!" Maurice declared.

Roxie turned up her nose at that suggestion. She wasn't into ribs. They were greasy and messy, and she didn't like eating with her fingers.

Maurice rarely made a fuss, giving into her whims and wishes most of the time so she decided to go along with him this time. She made reservations for eight.

The four couples met in the lobby of Barney's Barbecue the following Friday night. As the men and women chatted about their grandchildren and golf games and their Bridge scores, Roxie noticed that Maurice was nowhere in sight. She assumed he had gone to the men's room. Then she felt someone nudge her on the leg. She pulled back, only to be tapped again. She looked under the table...and there was Maurice crawling around, apparently looking for something.

Roxie bent down and whispered, "What are you doing?"

"My bridge came loose. I think it fell under the table."

Roxie was mortified. She opened her purse and pulled out a small flashlight she carried with her in order to find the keyhole in her car door or to light her path in the dark. She turned it on but nothing happened. The battery had run down.

Within moments the entire group became aware of the search and joined in, each one checking under seats and around the outside of the table.

A minute later Jake, who was sitting next to Maurice, stood up holding a strip of three teeth. Maurice was embarrassed but thankful. Roxie was relieved. "That's what can happen when you eat barbecued ribs. Tearing off the meat from the bone while wearing a bridge is not the best idea," she muttered to herself.

At the end of the evening Maurice surprised everyone, especially his wife. He stood up and raised his glass of cranberry juice. A toothless grin crossed his face.

"To Jake," he announced with uncharacteristic humor. "He wins the 'bridge' tournament tonight. I'm happy he was on my team."

Reflection

He will have no fear of bad news; his heart is steadfast, trusting in the LORD (Psalm 112:7).

Dear God, I know how embarrassing it can be to misplace important items, especially in front of others. Help me focus on and keep track of what is happening right now.

Key Moment

Ronnie swung into the parking lot in front of Babe's Burgers. She had spent five hours at the university library preparing for a history test. Now she was bleary from hunger and thirst. Maybe she was crazy after all to be going for a master's degree in world history at her age. At 55 years old she was the oldest student by far in her classes, but she wasn't going to let that stop her. She'd wanted this notch on her belt of achievements ever since she left college early more than 30 years before. She'd get her degree, by golly, even if it took every cell in her brain to make it happen!

She realized that studying into the night was not smart. She was fried—from too much time in the books and too little time in bed. But first she needed food. Ronnie dashed inside, ordered a burger, fries, and lemonade, and then wolfed them down like a starving teenager. She emptied her tray, visited the ladies' room, and returned to her car. She felt much better—still tired but at least fueled for the ride home.

Ronnie pulled out of the lot and turned right at the corner and moved into the lane that would put her on the highway toward home. She ran her tongue over her teeth. The onions on the burger tasted good, but they left her with telltale breath. She reached into her purse for a piece of gum or a mint. She always had a stash of one or the other in the bottom of her bag.

She searched with one hand while steering with the other. She dug around but she couldn't find a stray piece of gum—and no mints either.

Suddenly she panicked. Where were her car keys? She always put them in the zippered side pocket. It was empty. Her palms were suddenly damp, and she blinked in disbelief. What a time to lose her keys! She had two appointments the following day.

Ronnie pulled over to the side of the road to do a thorough search with her flashlight. She turned off the motor and in an instant broke out laughing. Her car keys were exactly where they belonged—in the ignition of the car she was driving!

Reflection

[There is] a time to weep and a time
to laugh (Ecclesiastes 3:4).

Dear God, you must surely get a kick out of some of my antics as I go through the golden years. I'd better laugh too or I'll sit down and cry.

Those Grandkids

Dot Org

I know a thing or two about computers and about websites. I've been in business for 35 years, and I feel good about my technical skills, given that I started with a manual typewriter and transitioned up to the latest Mac. I can Google, cut-and-paste, create an alias file, and retrieve a "lost" document with the best of 'em. But I can be knocked off my office chair by a four-year-old who will soon pass me by—perhaps even before he learns to read.

A few weeks ago my grandson came to visit. One of his favorite pastimes is to play on my computer. I have games and puzzles and cartoons, all kinds of fun stuff to entertain him for an hour at least. He knows the rules. No playing on the computer unless I'm with him. Being careful and gentle with the equipment. Following my instructions when a problem arises. With tech consulting and repair fees running more than $100 an hour, I don't want to risk him disabling or erasing some important program or messing with the system. So far so good.

I sat him on my lap during that visit, and he asked to play some games his sisters knew about on a particular website. I was familiar with what he wanted, but I couldn't remember the URL. I typed in a couple of different ones, hoping my mind would kick in and provide at least a hint. After a couple of minutes of listening to me saying, "Nope. Not yet. Haven't got it quite right. One more try..." Miles folded his arms across his chest and let out a big sigh. And there was no mistaking the tone of disgust that went with it.

"Grammy," the little one piped up in a loud voice, "PBSKIDS DOT O-R-G."

He got my attention. I typed it in and—presto!—we reached the portal to the games he wanted.

Sure enough, the golden years ain't for wimps! To keep up with four-year-old tech-savvy grandchildren one has to muster on or be set aside.

Reflection

Faith is being sure of what we hope for and certain
of what we do not see (Hebrews 11:1).

_____

Dear God, thank you that I can learn from the children in my life, just as they can learn from me...and I can learn from you.

Ice Queen

Betty turned the pages of an old photo album while gliding on the swing on her front porch. She fingered one picture of her and her father waltzing across the frozen pond by the family home when she was around eight. She remembered that day vividly. Dad had given up a Saturday morning on the farm to go skating with her for her birthday—the one gift she'd wanted.

Betty teared up when she looked at the stocking cap and gloves she was wearing. Her mother had given them to her that day so she'd stay warm while she skated. Later Betty and her dad returned home and curled up together in front of the fireplace and sipped hot chocolate and ate glazed donuts.

The phone rang, interrupting Betty's reverie. She laid the album on the glass side table and answered the call on the second ring. She was expecting to hear from her granddaughter Carrie. She listened for a moment and then spoke up. "All right, darling. I'll be there, but just for your birthday lunch, okay? I can't skate with you and your friends afterward. It's been years since I've even put on a pair of skates. I'll sit on the bench and cheer you on."

"But, Grams, you have to skate!" begged Carrie. "All my friends want to see you on the ice. It'll be fun. I'll hold your hand if you get scared. Besides the ice rink is really safe. No bumps...and there's a guy in a vest who skates around to make sure no one gets hurt."

Betty sighed and murmured a prayer, *Lord, did you set this up? Okay, I'll do it but I'm going to need one of your angel bodyguards.* Betty agreed to skate, and Carrie whooped with joy.

The following Saturday Betty met Carrie and her mother and Carrie's friends at the Westside Indoor Skating Rink. They ate lunch at the ringside tables and then went to the room where everyone changed into rental skates. They walked to the rink. As Betty stepped onto the ice her heart was pounding hard and her hands were sweaty with worry. She held on to the sideboard as she half-skated and half-walked around the rink. The second time she let go of the board and grasped Carrie's hand instead. By the third time her confidence returned, and she felt like a young girl again. She skated out to the center of the rink and began making figure eights on the ice.

Then she did something she hadn't done in years. She held up one leg and steadied herself on the other, arms outstretched—but not for long. The next thing Betty knew she was flat on her back-side, feet up in the air. How embarrassing! Carrie and her friends rushed over to check on her. "You all right, Grams?" Carrie pulled Betty to her feet.

Just then the kid in the orange vest with STAFF printed across the front zoomed over and asked if Betty needed a doctor or an aspirin or an ambulance. He sounded scared.

Betty didn't like attention, but this kind of attention was the worst kind. "I'm fine," she muttered. "My granddaughter said her friends wanted to see me on ice, and I didn't want to disappoint them."

Reflection

Be strong and take heart,
all you who hope in the LORD (Psalm 31:24).

———————————

Lord, I'm so thankful I can participate in life, regardless of the little mishaps.

Friend or Foe?

Pat and Jack took their grandson Willie to the local shopping mall the second week in December. They were excited to show the four-year-old all the Christmas decorations, the giant tree in the plaza, and of course Santa Claus in his snug little house atop a mound of faux snow.

This tradition had been in their family for 30 years. Each of their children had visited Santa, and now it was fun for Pat and Jack to take their grandson. A photographer stood to the side, and as each child approached Santa and popped up on his knee, the woman snapped a picture and then handed a ticket to the parents or grandparents in case they wished to purchase the photo at the sales booth.

The whole thing was a bit commercial for Pat's taste, but still, seeing Santa was part of the family tradition. She would overlook the photo opportunity and focus on watching the delight on Willie's face when his turn came to tell Santa the special toys he was hoping to receive Christmas Day.

After standing in line for 30 minutes amid fidgety children, crying babies, and exhausted moms and dads, it was finally Willie's turn to sit on Santa's knee. Willie looked at Pat and frowned. She nudged him forward with a nod and a smile. "Go on, honey. It's your turn. Tell Santa what you'd like him to bring you for Christmas."

Jack took out his own camera and stepped up to take the perfect picture at just the right moment.

Willie climbed onto Santa's lap and looked up at the jolly man with the long white beard. The boy didn't say a word.

"And what can I bring you, young man?" Santa asked jovially.

Willie still didn't say a word.

"Speak up, honey," called Pat.

"It's all right, Willie," added Jack.

Willie jumped down and leaned over the little fence that separated him from his grandparents. "I can't tell him," Willie whispered.

"Why not?" asked Pat. "What are you waiting for?"

"Gramma, you told me never to talk to strangers, remember?"

Reflection

Whoever humbles himself like this child is the
greatest in the kingdom of heaven (Matthew 18:4).

Lord, sometimes I treat you like a stranger. I don't talk to you or listen to you. Let me change that today. I want to start each day in prayer and praise with you.

Heaven Can Wait

One day while Charlene was visiting her daughter and family, she took her young grandson, David, on a bike ride/walk. He rode and she walked alongside. "I reviewed the rules of the road with him before starting," Charlene commented. " I knew his penchant for doing things his way. I reminded him to stop at the corner, look both ways, and then wait for me before crossing with his bike. He agreed, but not for long.

"The next thing I knew he had darted out on the busy street without stopping or looking. I ran after him, breathless with worry, and shouted in my loudest voice, 'David, you get back here right now! You're in trouble!'

"When he returned, I challenged him about the rule I had just enforced and told him how terrible it would be if he died in a crash."

David responded, "Don't worry. If I die I'll go straight to heaven."

Charlene admired his confidence...even though she was ticked off at the same time. "He was too quick to dismiss my concern and my authority," she asserted. However, she soon descended from her high horse when the Lord caught her attention.

Doesn't that sound familiar? he asked.

"Oops! I had to admit it did ring a bell—though ever so faintly. Do I rush ahead when God asks me to stay back? Do I defy his authority when he instructs me for my own welfare? Do I mouth off when it's my place to be silent and listen? Yes, I had to admit I did from time to time."

Charlene wilted for a moment and then held up her head and asked the Lord to give her another chance to show she loves him. She said that even if she disobeys she knows she'll go to heaven, for Jesus has claimed her as his own and she has accepted his sacrifice for her sin. "But," she asked, "is that any way to behave toward my God and Lord who gave me life?"

Reflection

Keep my decrees and laws, for the man
who obeys them will live by them.
I am the LORD (Leviticus 18:5).

———————

God, thank you for being the God of a second and third and fourth chance...and even more. You always give me more and better than I deserve. Help me keep my eyes on you all the days of my life.

Senior Curfew

Thirteen-year-old P.D. spent Tuesday night with his grandparents while his folks were out of town for a business meeting. He had a geography project due at school the following morning. His mom didn't have time to run him to the store for the few remaining items he needed, but she assured him that Grandma or Grandpa wouldn't mind taking him.

P.D. wasn't as sure of this as his mother was. He knew from past experience that Grandma and Grandpa Jones were the early to bed, early to rise types so he couldn't imagine them taking him to the store at night. But he didn't drive yet so he had to rely on them.

"Grandma," he said after dinner while the two cleared the table and stacked the dishes, "I have to buy a couple things at Porter's for a homework assignment due tomorrow."

Grandma looked up. She didn't smile. "What's this? You wait until seven to tell us? What makes you think we're going to go to the store at this late hour?"

P.D. had his reasons, so he took a deep breath and blurted them out. "Well, I didn't get here till five. You said Grandpa would be home at five-thirty, we'd eat dinner at six, and you wanted to go to bed by eight sharp." Grandma was listening so P.D. kept on going. "I thought

194

seven would be the perfect time. It takes ten minutes to drive to the store, and ten minutes home. That gives us thirty minutes to shop. We'll be back by ten minutes to eight. That gives you enough time to shower and still be in bed by your curfew—eight o'clock."

Grandma Jones was speechless. How could she argue with such a logical and thoughtful individual? She smiled and winked at her grandson. "Grab your jacket. I'll get the car."

Reflection

Prepare your minds for action (1 Peter 1:13).

Lord, these kids keep me on my toes and in my car. It's good to be alive and to share these golden years with them.

Cold Shoulder

Deedee offered to drive her 16-year-old grandson, Skip, to basketball practice and to stay and watch him play. She hadn't seen him in action for some time, so she looked forward to it. Skip was eager to have an audience, and he was happy for her invitation to have dinner together afterward.

Deedee picked up Skip Wednesday after school. It was a particularly brisk day, but she didn't pay much attention to the weather until she was in the car and remembered she'd left her heavy sweater on the bed in her rush to get out the door.

Skip, on the other hand, was always hot. He was 6' 2" with a strong build and good circulation so he liked to ride with the windows rolled down most, if not all, of the way.

"Skip, please roll up the window," Deedee asked. "I'm already freezing, and we're not even on the freeway yet. Puleeze!" she teased.

Skip let out a big sigh and rolled it up—a little—but not enough to make any difference.

Deedee rubbed her arms, hoping Skip would take the hint and comply with her simple request.

"All the way *up!*" she commanded. "And I mean now!"

He rolled it up another inch or two.

Exasperated, Deedee explained, "I know I should have brought my sweater. But I didn't. I was in a hurry to pick you up and forgot it. And so now I'm asking you to close the window the entire way!"

Skip let out another sigh, but he followed his grandmother's instructions. He should have known from experience that he was pushing her a bit too far. Apparently he couldn't resist spilling what was on his mind. "All right," he said. "But you seem cranky. I think you need a nap."

That did it. Deedee toppled over the edge. "You're absolutely right!" she snapped. "I do need a nap." That said, she turned at the next corner and headed back where they had come from. "I'll just drop you at school," she added. "You can call your mom 'cause I'm taking your advice and heading home for a nap."

Reflection

Let us not become conceited, provoking and
envying each other (Galatians 5:26).

---

*Thank you, God, that I can speak up when I need to. Help
me do it in a gentle, reasonable way.*

A Matter of Comfort

Six-year-old Matty enjoyed spending time with his 60-something-year-old grandfather, Anthony, whom Matty called Pappy. The two were like jam and bread. They were better together.

One Saturday morning Pappy invited Matty to go car shopping with him. "Not sure if I'll buy one today, but I'm gonna look and see what's around. And I need your advice," Pappy said. "Two heads are better than one."

Matty was happy that it was his head Pappy had chosen. He did have some ideas, all right. He liked cars without tops. He thought it would be fun to race down the highway with the wind blowing his hair. His friends would think it was cool if they could ride with him in a top-down car. Yep. He'd try to talk Pappy into buying one.

The pair drove from one car dealership to another. Pappy test-drove a few models but none appealed to Matty. He had a picture in his mind of the kind of car he wanted Pappy to buy. He pointed to a few, but before he could comment about what fun it to would be to drive one, Pappy squelched the idea. "Nothing low and fast for me," Pappy asserted. "Just a nice-sized, comfortable car. That's what I have in mind."

"But Pappy," Matty pleaded after they'd visited no fewer than five car lots, "we saw a bunch of cars just like that and you said no to every one of them. Look!" he said, pointing to a shiny blue car in the corner of the parking lot. "There's another one."

Pappy craned his neck and squinted in the afternoon sun. "That's a convertible, Matty."

"But isn't that what you said you wanted? A 'nice-sized comfertible car'?"

Pappy laughed out loud.

Matty wasn't sure what was so funny. He frowned and looked off to the side. Grandpas were kind of weird sometimes. They say one thing and do something else.

Reflection

Children's children are a crown
to the aged (Proverbs 17:6).

Lord, sometimes there is more than an age gap between grandparents and grandchildren. There's also a communication gap! Thanks to your grace, we're able to bridge that gap when it needs a bit of repair.

Silly
Stuff

Fantastic!

"Claire, the dryer won't shut off!"

Claire rushed out of the bedroom, down the hall, and into the laundry room.

"What are you talking about? This is a brand-new machine."

"I'm telling you," shouted her husband, Brad, "the contraption keeps going and going. I don't know what happened. I tossed in a load of clothes and now...well, listen for yourself."

Claire opened the door of the dryer. The drum was still. No motion whatsoever, and yet she could hear a peculiar hum in the background. How unnerving. One more thing to handle in a week that was already bulging with problems and challenges.

Brad looked at his watch. "Too late for a repair call now. We'll have to get on it in the morning. It's a good thing it's under warranty."

"Wait!" Claire snapped her fingers. "The circuit breaker box. Let's try to shut it off by tripping the breaker. At least that way we won't be in any danger from something overheating or shorting out."

"Great idea!" Brad opened the metal box and ran his finger down the names of appliances and rooms. When he reached "dryer" he clicked the switch to OFF. But nothing changed. The faint hum persisted.

Claire felt her pulse jump. It was nearly ten. They were about to go to bed for much-needed sleep and now this. She tapped Brad on the arm. "Let's pray about this. We need Holy Spirit wisdom and peace to get through the night."

The couple prayed and then headed for bed. But first Brad propped open the door to the dryer in case it might overheat while they were asleep.

The next morning, after a fitful night with Claire up and down checking to see if she smelled smoke, Brad called the appliance company. The service rep was confounded. She'd never heard of a dryer not shutting off, especially when someone tripped the breaker. She made an appointment for a technician to come out right away because this sounded like an emergency.

That afternoon a young man in a blue work jacket with the name "Jason" sewed on the front pocket showed up at their door. He pulled out the dryer, checked all points, and tinkered with this and that while Claire and Brad stood by nearly holding their breath. Then he stood up and shook his head from side to side. "This dryer is in perfect condition," he said. "I don't know what to tell you. I hear the noise too, but it's not the dryer, you can be sure of that."

Claire's voice bumped up an octave from her usual range. "No, we can't!" she blurted. "I've been up half the night with worry. You can't leave until you help us. What are we going to do? I have company coming this week, and we'll have extra laundry for days."

Jason heaved a sigh, and then brushed his hand over a set of switches next to the counter on the right side of the dryer. Click. Click. Click. The moment he touched the third one, the whirring noise ceased—just like that.

"What did you do?" Claire asked.

"Touched these switches. Not sure why. But it looks like this third switch is a fan of some kind," the young man said. "I don't know where it goes, but it doesn't have anything to do with the dryer."

Claire slumped against the wall behind her. "Thank you. I'm totally embarrassed but completely thankful too."

Brad's face turned pink.

"Honey?" Claire asked.

"I'm the culprit," he admitted. "Guess I bumped the switch when I opened the cabinet above."

The three had a good laugh as Jason packed up his toolbox. "There's no charge," the young repairman said.

Brad reached into his pocket, pulled out a ten-dollar bill, and pressed it into Jason's free hand. "Have a Coke and a sandwich on us. We're heading back to bed for a good day's sleep."

Reflection

Make every effort to add to your faith goodness;
and to goodness, knowledge (2 Peter 1:5).

———————————

Lord, leave it to me to jump to conclusions—and usually the worst possible ones. How much better off I'd be if I turned to you first and asked for your guidance. I'm so glad you bear with me and come to my rescue—always with a fantastic solution.

Keep Out!

Hollis is a private person...really private. His wife, Carmen, can attest to that. He works at home in a small room he refers to as "*my* office," and he likes it that way. When he and Carmen take off for a few days, Hollis locks the room up tight. Although it may seem a bit odd to some people since the couple lock their front door before leaving, Hollis prefers this double-lock system.

One week in July they agreed to let some friends from another city stay overnight in their upstairs condo while they were away. Hollis was a bit anxious about having people inside while they were gone, but Carmen reminded him of how upstanding the Walkers were. "Not to worry," she said. "Put anything you're concerned about in the office. When you lock it, they'll know that room is off-limits."

Hollis agreed and they made plans for their weekend in the desert. Carmen went into town to run a few last-minute errands the day before they left. Hollis remained behind to organize his office and lock it up. He hid the key so there would be no temptation on the visitors' part to steal a glance.

Later that day he remembered something he wanted from the office but couldn't recall where he'd hidden the key. *Drat! What a way to start a vacation,* he thought. He didn't want to admit his lapse of memory to Carmen, so while she was away he pulled the extension ladder out of the garage and propped it against the side of the house. He climbed up, pried open the window to his office, jockeyed through, grabbed the item he wanted, and then walked out the door. It worked like a charm.

The next day he and Carmen packed their car and backed down the driveway. That evening they checked in with the Walkers to make sure the couple had arrived safely, found the house key behind the azalea bush, and were comfortably settled inside. Indeed they were and very grateful for Hollis and Carmen's hospitality.

Three days later Hollis and Carmen returned home. Hollis had remembered while they were away that he hid the key to his office in a little box in a drawer under his workbench in the garage. He grabbed it and proceeded into the house. But he didn't need it after all. The door to the office was unlocked and slightly ajar. As he walked into the room, the window was wide open too. He looked outside and a ladder was propped up to it on the outside. He panicked. Someone had broken in!

He ran to tell Carmen when suddenly it hit him. *He* was the burglar! He had opened the window when he climbed the ladder to enter the office for the missing item. And he had walked out the door, leaving it unlocked and open. He had been in so much of a hurry to get going that he'd forgotten to close the window, shut the door, and put the ladder away.

Hollis felt his face grow warm with embarrassment. He shut the window and locked it. He then snuck downstairs to grab the ladder. Now if he could just return it to the garage before Carmen started asking questions...

Too late! There she stood.

"Planning to fix something?" she asked.

Hollis mumbled something about trying to cover his tracks.

Reflection

You will lift up your face without
shame (Job 11:15).

---

*Dear God, thank you for not holding my weaknesses against
me.*

Splash of Color

Chip and Dodi were expecting company for dinner. While Dodi put the finishing touches on the pork roast and whipped potatoes, Chip agreed to give their house the once-over before their guests arrived. He ran a feather duster over the blinds and furniture, swept the kitchen floor, and gathered a few stray items on the counter in the hallway to put them away. Suddenly the doorbell rang. Their neighbors had arrived.

Chip panicked. His arms were full so he did the first thing that came to mind. He tossed the slacks, blouse, and miscellaneous T-shirts and socks into the washing machine and shut the door. They probably needed washing anyway, so he was a step ahead of himself. He'd take care of them in the morning. He closed the folding door that hid the machine and joined their company.

Dodi served a delicious meal topped off with homemade apple pie and whipped cream. The couples played a few rounds of Shanghai and then said goodnight. Chip and Dodi headed for bed, tired but relaxed after a lovely evening.

The following morning, Dodi called from the bedroom. "Chip, please put the guest towels and our bath towels in the washing machine and turn it on, okay? I'll be out in a minute."

"Sure thing." Chip tossed the towels in, added soap and a splash of bleach, and turned on the machine. Then he called goodbye as he left for a round of golf.

Later that day Dodi went to transfer the clothes to the dryer. She pulled out the load and gasped. There were Chip's brand-new, caramel-colored corduroy slacks a new shade of ghastly orange! Next she picked up her black knit blouse with the hand-embroidered flowers. Ruined.

"Bleach!" She knew it.

Chip waltzed in the door after his game, humming a little tune. He had lowered his score by a couple of points, and he was feeling great...until Dodi broke the news. He could hardly believe it. Then he remembered what he'd done the night before. When he tossed in the towels earlier that day, he'd done so without thinking or looking. The black blouse, tan slacks, and white towels got washed—and bleached—together.

Chip hung his head. "I'm so sorry and embarrassed. I'll make it up to you, I promise. How about lunch at the mall—after we do a bit of necessary shopping."

Dodi smiled. "Looks like this is working out pretty well, after all."

Reflection

Let me not be put to shame, O LORD,
for I have cried out to you (Psalm 31:17).

Dear God, I thank you that I can forgive other people's mistakes and even laugh at their foibles...along with my own. I can't afford to take life too seriously, especially during these golden years.

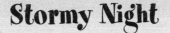

Stormy Night

Cathy quit driving when she turned 60. She'd been in two frightening accidents, so she gave up the wheel and hasn't looked back. Well, that's not entirely true. According to her husband, Mike, she still drives—from the passenger seat. He laughs when he tells this story. Cathy does not. She believes it's her job to keep them alive, so she pays attention to every detail—from left and right turns to traffic lights and detours.

One morning after a horrific blizzard had dumped a foot of snow and sleet on the nearby city and country roads, Cathy panicked. She hadn't heard from Mike for several hours, and he was driving home from a sales call about two hours south of their home. She called her neighbor Sunny and voiced her fear. "I should have gone with him," she moaned into the phone. "Mike doesn't see as well as I do…"

Sunny chuckled and then apologized. "I'm not making fun of this situation, Cathy, but come on. Mike is not going to die when he can only drive about 10 miles per hour in this stuff. You know Mike. He wouldn't do anything risky."

Cathy poured out her anxiety. "Accidents happen even at 10 miles per hour. I tell you, I'm scared!"

"Where's your faith?"

211

"I have faith in the power of the blizzard. Have you ever been in one? It can be terrifying."

Sunny persisted. "I'm talking about faith in *God*. He knows all about this. He'll take care of Mike, and he'll take care of you. Have you prayed about this? Ask for protection and courage."

"Well, what can God do about a blizzard anyway?"

Within a moment Cathy dissolved into laughter. What had she just said? She calmed down. "Correction! He can do whatever he wants, I know. I *will* pray."

"Amen!" Sunny declared. "So relax. God is in charge."

Reflection

I would hurry to my place of shelter, far from the
tempest and storm (Psalm 55:8).

————————————

Dear God, thank you for being with me during the storms of life—and during the seasons of sunshine and flowers too.

Make That an LT

Dotty and her friend Elise planned a picnic lunch as part of their drive up the west coast where the two wanted to look at some vacation rentals for a getaway with their husbands the following summer. The two couples were going to celebrate their fortieth wedding anniversaries together.

Elise picked up Dotty at eight-thirty sharp, and the two took turns behind the wheel until ten-thirty, when they stopped for a cold drink and a bathroom break. At noon they parked along the ocean near a small picnic grove. The sun was shining, the air crisp but not cold, and the sky a perfect blue. They chose a table next to a broad pine tree and pulled out the basket of goodies.

Dotty brought lemonade and her chocolate swirl cookies, and Elise unpacked the ingredients for the sandwiches and a bag of chips for each one. She also opened a glass container with fresh cherries.

Dotty looked on, her mouth watering with hunger. Elise was famous for her creative sandwiches. Dotty expected fresh guacamole, homegrown tomatoes, a spicy sauce, maybe even roasted turkey or smoked salmon.

Elise laid out the focaccia bread, juicy tomato slices, and red-leaf lettuce—Dotty's favorite. "We're having BLTs today." Elise smiled while pulling out her mini grill for the bacon and a small cup of mayo.

Dotty couldn't believe her friend. She thinks of everything! Even a portable grill for cooking bacon. *I wish I were as thoughtful and organized as she is.* Suddenly Elise's face turned white. She checked under the picnic table, rummaged through the picnic basket, and even plowed through her purse. "I know it's here somewhere," she mumbled.

"What?" Dotty was bursting with curiosity.

Elise looked up and opened her palms. "The 'B' as in bacon! I can't find it anywhere. She looked off in the distance, trying to remember when she'd last seen it. She laughed out loud. "I know exactly where it is. On Ted's workbench in the garage. I took it out of the fridge at the last moment, intending to add it to the other ingredients. I laid it down for a second while I pulled the basket off the shelf over the workbench." Elise sighed. "What else is new? These golden years are getting to me, Dotty. Sure glad you're in them with me."

The women had a good laugh and sat down to enjoy their LT sandwiches.

Reflection

You will surely forget your trouble, recalling it only
as waters gone by (Job 11:16).

Dear God, as long as I have you—the Bread of Life—I'm in good shape no matter what happens.

Brake for the Bathroom

Honey, I don't think I can hold it another minute." Chet squeezed his legs together, and the car jerked as he lifted his foot off the accelerator.

Ethel panicked. She'd been through this before. Chet was nearing the age when he might be safer wearing adult diapers. But then she thought of what a blow it would be to his ego. Incontinence was just one of the woes that sometimes tarnished the happy golden years. Sometimes Chet could handle himself successfully for weeks, even a month or more, and then suddenly finding the bathroom—especially if they were away from home—became an emergency. This was one of those times.

They were on their way to their favorite mall. It was time to update Chet's wardrobe and have a nice lunch at their favorite cafe. As they drove down the freeway, Ethel noticed they were two exits away from the off-ramp. But Chet couldn't wait. This was it. He needed to go—and he meant now.

There wasn't a gas station or fast-food sign in sight. *Dear God,* Ethel prayed, *please help us. I'm afraid Chet's not going to make it—and we don't have a change of clothes with us.*

Just then Ethel saw a port-a-potty on the median strip between the slow lane and an on-ramp. *One blue metal closet by the side of a busy road? How amazing!*

"Chet, quick. Pull over. Look! Just ahead. There's a toilet. Must be for the freeway work crew. I'm sure you can use it without a problem."

Chet glanced to his right, slid onto the shoulder, slowed down, and stopped the car right next to the cubicle. He flashed his blinkers, jumped out of the car, and dashed into the enclosure. Ethel kept an eye on the traffic and held her breath.

Seconds later Chet appeared, obviously relieved in more ways than one. He slid back into the driver's seat, checked traffic, and off they went—ready for that nice lunch and shopping. Ethel shouted a prayer of gratitude, "Thank you, Lord!"

Reflection

Walk in the way the LORD your God has commanded you (Deuteronomy 5:33).

Dear Lord, you even care about the intimate things. That becomes so important as I grow older. You always provide when there appears to be no hope and often in the nick of time. Thank you for meeting my every need in the most perfect way.

Where Credit Is Due

olly simply didn't have a head for numbers. She knew it. Her husband knew it. Her daughter knew it. Her banker knew it. But sometimes a person simply has to push through his or her weakness to discover a new strength. Dolly decided one day that enough was enough. She was not a dumb, gray-head-dyed-blond who couldn't add two plus two. She would change her image of herself and the image her husband and daughter and banker had of her.

Dolly opened the topic of finances with her husband, Wilbur, over coffee and strawberry waffles one Monday morning in February. "Honey," she cooed, "may I please assume a little more fiscal responsibility? After all, we're getting older and I need to be prepared—you know, in case you go first."

Wilbur lowered his glasses and looked at Dolly over the top of them. He grunted. "All right. I guess today is as good as any. I'd like you to transfer $5000 by phone from our savings account to our household checking account. Write a check for $4000 for our property taxes and drop it into the mail. And pay off the $1000 balance at Maxie's."

Wilbur explained each step to Dolly one more time. Dolly made a few notes, nodded, and set to work. She called the bank and transferred the money from savings to checking. A few clicks on

217

the phone keypad, and she received a message saying "transaction complete."

Dolly jumped up. She had scored. No one was more surprised than she was. She had been convinced for so long that she couldn't handle a bank account, but she was already proving she could. She felt so empowered!

Next she sat down at the desk in the den and wrote the $4000 check and the one for $1000. She popped them both in the mailbox on the corner. She clapped one hand against the other and smiled broadly. Piece of cake!

Ten days later two envelopes arrived in the mail. One was from the county clerk's office saying she was delinquent by $3000 for their property tax, and the other said she had made an overpayment of $3000 on her clothing account at Maxie's. The store accounts manager would issue her a refund check for the sum, and it would arrive in three to six weeks. *By then,* Dolly worried, *I might be in the clinker for property tax evasion!*

Dolly broke into tears and confessed her crime to Wilbur. First he barked at her and then laughed out loud. "Don't worry," he said. "I'll visit you every day in jail." A moment later he put his arms around her and told her he'd take care of the problem the next day. Fortunately they had another savings account with funds for a rainy day. And this day certainly qualified. Dolly handed over the checkbook and said she'd stick to knitting.

Reflection

Keep your lives free from the love of money and be
content with what you have (Hebrews 13:5).

---

*Dear God, I am grateful you look after my financial needs
as well as my spiritual ones.*

Hold the Sprouts

Sid had just about had it with the folks at Eddie's Deli. He couldn't get a simple ham sandwich on rye anymore. With the advent of all the healthy choice items, it took him 30 minutes just to get through the menu board. Custom breads, imported cheeses, organic dressings, spring greens, soy mayo, radish sprouts. What was a hungry man to do? He looked for familiar words such as lettuce, as in "head of," and mayo, as in "mayonnaise," white bread, as in "Wonder," but no, Eddie had gone the way of the other goofballs in the sandwich business. He'd obviously bought into all the baloney about low salt, low fat, low calorie, which in Sid's opinion equaled low taste...make that no taste.

Sid liked Eddie, however, so he didn't want to ditch the guy after 20 years of patronage. On the other hand, he wasn't going to be some pansy. He liked a good steak and greasy fries at least once a week, even though he could almost see the eyes of his dear departed wife, Connie, staring at him through the clouds.

One Friday at noon Sid walked into Eddie's. He decided to give the owner another chance. Maybe if he asked for what he wanted, he could get it. No harm in trying.

"Make that a plain ham sandwich on regular rye," he said when the clerk took his order.

"Sorry, sir, but we only have what's on the menu board." She pointed to the Country Cousins Ham Special, which had a line of ingredients longer than Sid's "to do" list: "cured ham, imported honey mustard, select spring greens, vine-ripe tomatoes, Bermuda onion slices, and fresh, organic alfalfa sprouts." Sid nearly gagged when he read the last item. *Alfalfa? Isn't that what farmers feed their horses and cattle?* But he was hungry and it was too late to go elsewhere. He got an idea...one he hoped would work. "All right, young lady—Sheila—you talked me into it. I'll have the Country Cousins Ham Special."

The young woman smiled. "Very good, sir. I think you'll enjoy it. It's new on our menu and very popular. I'll have that ready in just a moment. Rye or home-baked, 10-grain bread?"

Sid smiled politely. "Rye, please."

As Sheila began to assemble the ingredients, Sid poked his head over the glass-enclosed counter and issued orders as if he were a colonel in charge of a military unit.

"Hold the imported honey mustard."

The girl nodded.

"And the same for spring greens."

Sheila dropped the greens back into the container.

"Ditto for the vine-ripe tomato," called Sid. "And skip the Bermuda onion slice. Now if it were grown in the good old U.S. of A. I might decide otherwise."

Sheila blinked. "Sir?"

Poor kid. She doesn't get it.

"Oh and hold those sprouty things. Whew! For a minute I thought you were going to slip those past me."

Sheila enclosed the two slices of bread with the ham in the center in a paper wrap, taped it shut, and handed it to Sid. "That'll be $5.95, sir. Will that be all?"

"Yes, that's all."

Sid slapped a $10 bill on the counter. "Keep the change, young lady. I appreciate your making a custom sandwich just for me." He picked up his ham on rye and strode out the door. He decided he just might keep giving Eddie his business after all.

Reflection

For the kingdom of God is not a matter of eating and drinking, but of righteousness, peace and joy in the Holy Spirit (Romans 14:17).

God, I praise you that life is not about food and drink but about praise and worship and obedience to your holy will.

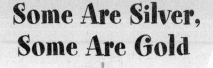

Some Are Silver, Some Are Gold

Dan and Carol decided to go to their fiftieth high school reunion in Lexington, Kentucky. The closer the day came, the more eager they got—especially Carol.

"I hope my old friends recognize me," she commented one night over dinner.

Dan gazed into her eyes. "Of course they will. You were the prettiest girl in our class then and you still are. I don't have to see anyone else to know that."

"Wow!" Tears tugged at Carol's eyes. "What a nice thing to say." Still, she wasn't so sure. She looked in the mirror each morning, and all she saw were new signs of aging—the soft folds that had taken over her once-firm neck, eyelids that sagged a bit unless she made an effort to keep her eyes wide open, hair thinning a bit in front despite her attempts to "tease" it into place.

"I have an idea," Dan offered. "Let's haul out the old albums and look at a few pictures so we'll remember names and faces. It's been a long time since we saw most of these people."

Carol laughed. "Are you kidding? Our classmates won't look anything like they did 50 years ago. I don't see the point in..."

It was too late for protests. Dan had already hauled out the albums and yearbooks. He paged through them with keen interest. Carol noticed him pause here and there, point and chuckle, and then move on. She couldn't resist. Soon she was sitting beside him laughing and reminiscing with him.

Steve Krajecki smiled off the page with his blunt-cut hair and T-shirt with sleeves rolled up to his armpits. He had been a real character. Belinda's photo was next. Her bouffant hairdo and off-the-shoulder blouse said it all. She was the class flirt. Carol and Dan remembered one person after another. Then they came across their pictures. Good place to stop and talk. Carol was dismayed at how pretty she'd been. She never thought so then. If only she could pluck those good looks off the page now!

Dan had changed too...but not that much. He was still her handsome hero, even more so after 45 years of marriage and the ups and downs of a very full life together.

They closed the books. Then Dan pulled down an album with photos of themselves and their neighborhood friends from years ago. They'd lived beside some of the couples for more than 30 years. They'd watched each other's kids grow up.

Carol paused and then poked Dan in the ribs. "Dan, who are these good-looking young people with our children?"

He looked and poked her back. "Not sure about the woman, but the guy is me." He patted his soft belly, ran a hand through his thinning hair, and adjusted his glasses. "I haven't changed a bit, have I?"

Carol rolled her eyes. "Not a bit, darling. You're still a legend in your own mind! And every woman at the reunion will agree with you. I'm just glad you've chosen to take me as your date...and mate."

Reflection

Though outwardly we are wasting away, yet
inwardly we are being renewed day by day
(2 Corinthians 4:16).

---

*Lord God, thank you that what really matters is how I take
care of my soul...through you.*

The Pampered Camper

Raymond didn't ask much out of life—certainly not during the golden years. He felt more blessed than he deserved just to be where he was—retired with a comfortable income and good health, give or take a few aches and pains. He was still able to hit the ball over the net in his weekly tennis game with his lifelong friend Hal, and at the end of the day he enjoyed a hearty meal, some conversation, and a nice cuddle with Kate, his wife of 49 years.

If he were pressed hard, he'd admit there was one thing missing... something he wanted to do with Kate. And that was camping in Mammoth, California, a mere three-hour drive from their home near Carson City, Nevada. But Kate had dug in the heels of her hiking boots long ago. She'd hike by day, by golly, but camping was out of the question. She wanted to know that when the sun went down she could go up to her house on the hill and take a long, hot shower and sleep under the feathers of her down comforter all night long. No scary bears to worry her, no owls hooting outside a tent, no raccoons or ground squirrels or mosquitoes to contend with. And best of all, she could plug in her coffee maker in the morning and grab a carton of fresh cream in the nearby fridge. No way, José (or Raymond), was she going to budge from her position.

Raymond knew this in his gut, but he couldn't hold on to it in his heart. He was sure he could win her over. It was his dream, and he was going to do his best to turn it into reality. He understood why she thought camping was a drag when they had little kids. Too much work for too little reward in her mind. But their children were adults now with lives of their own. It was just the two of them, and it would be so, well, so romantic and peaceful to be in the quiet of nature, together under the canopy of a tent, holding on to one another on a starlit night.

If only he knew how to make such an adventure appealing to his pampered wife. He was certain that if he could get her out in the wild, she'd fall in love with it. The Alpenglow on the mountains just before sunset would take her breath away, and the fields of White Heather, Elephant's Head, Mountain Laurel, and Indian Paint Brush would invade her senses like nothing else.

Raymond relished his dream and held to it with praise and prayer. God said he'd give his children the desires of their hearts, so Raymond wasn't about to doubt the Lord now. He said nothing more about it to Kate for the rest of the year.

Then something quite amazing occurred the following March. On the fourteenth, the day of his seventieth birthday, someone propped an envelope with his name on it against his computer screen. He looked at the handwriting. It was Kate's. *How like her,* he mused, *to be the first one to wish me a happy birthday with a special Hallmark card.* Kate herself was the hallmark of thoughtfulness.

He opened it eagerly and there in front of his eyes was an invitation to go "pamping" at Sunset Camp near Mammoth, California—"the elegant way to spend a day or a week in the wild with the one you love." After reading the headline, he opened the brochure to pictures of "couple cabins" with skylights for viewing the starry nights, showers after a long day of hiking and sightseeing, coffee makers, a small fridge for snacks and drinks, and breakfast and lunch served in a dining hall overlooking the mountains. Brown-box lunches would be provided on request. The best part of all was the receipt for payment for the first week in August tucked into the brochure!

Raymond's eyes clouded as he took it in. God had provided. And apparently he had spoken to Kate about it. Just then his wife crept into the room and slipped her arms around his shoulders. "I hope you'll consider it," she said. "As you know from living with me for 49 years, I've always dreamed of going 'pamping' with you."

Reflection

A heart at peace gives life to
the body (Proverbs 14:30).

Lord, it is such a blessing when I can respond with love and enthusiasm to the needs and wishes of my mate. May I remember to do so when my spouse has a special yearning I can fulfill.

Wedding Gifts

Dan picked up the phone on the first ring. "Dad? Great to hear from you. What's new?"

"Last night Margie said 'yes.'"

"Yes to what?" Dan's heart pounded. His father was full of surprises. He wondered what he was up to now.

"Yes, she'd marry me. Isn't that great?"

"Well, sure. I mean if that's what you want. But, Dad, aren't you a bit..."

"Old? Go ahead and say it." Dan's father was clearly irritated. His voice rose and his breathing escalated.

"Well, yeah, kind of. I mean, Dad, you're 89 and Margie is 88. Are you sure you want to start the whole marriage thing all over again? How about just being friends? You have your set ways and she has hers...and where will you live? You each have a house. Dad, I'm just trying to be practical."

"Are you finished?"

"No, but it sounds as if you hope I am." Dan switched the phone to his other ear and took a swig of water as his father carried on about the wedding day he and Margie were planning for the fall.

"I suppose you think we might not live long enough to make it worthwhile. Is that what you're thinking? Be straight with me, son."

"Well, now that you mention it, yes. It had crossed my mind. Marriage is a big thing at any age, but in your late 80s it's even bigger. There's money to think about, and housing, and relationships, and what about health issues?"

"I think I'll hang up now. You're too negative for me."

"Dad, wait!" Dan broke into a sweat. "I'm sorry. I was just trying to be helpful. You know, like the way you were when Sue and I announced our engagement."

"If I remember correctly you didn't take my advice, so I guess I wasn't all that helpful."

Dan felt his face flush. His dad was right. He and Sue got married at 20 even though it wasn't the smartest decision they'd ever made. They were still in college at the time.

"Got your point, Dad. This is your life and your decision. I'm going to be happy for you and Margie, I promise. How about this?" He changed the tone in his voice. "What can Sue and I get you for a wedding present? You probably have everything you need between the two of you. Don't need a coffee maker or a toaster, right?" Dan laughed, trying to ease the tension.

"Actually there are quite a few things we'll need eventually, if not right away, so we're going to sign up with a bridal registry."

Dan slapped his forehead. He thought his dad had really lost it now. "You're what? Where? And what could you possibly need?"

"Medicine for memory and arthritis. Vitamins for vitality. Margie could use a walker. She's a little unsteady on her feet. We might need a wheelchair someday. And of course it's good to have a supply of bandages for cuts, a spare pair of reading glasses in case we break the ones we have, maybe a package or two of Depends—just in case—and a hearing booster for the phone. Don't need it yet, but my hearing isn't what it used to be."

Dan didn't know whether to laugh or moan. This was the most absurd list of wedding presents he'd ever heard. "And where do you think you'll find a bridal registry that sells all that?"

Dan's father was ready with an answer. "Community Pharmacy

on Second Street. We're going in today to sign up! Well, son, you asked what's new and that's about it. Sorry I don't have more to tell you, but at my age life is pretty much the same from day to day. Let's talk again soon."

Reflection

Wives, submit to your husbands, as is fitting in the Lord. Husbands, love your wives and do not be harsh with them (Colossians 3:18-19).

Dear God, this is pretty funny, but also pretty true. Old age has its unique set of circumstances that require a sense of humor if I'm going to get through them. Thank you for the grace to do so.

Who's in My Bed?

Bonnie set her teacup down and turned to her husband. "I know it's a challenge, Ralph, but I want to keep Mom and Dad home with us as long as possible. Are you with me on this?"

Ralph let out a deep breath and glanced at the photo of his in-laws on the wall above the kitchen table. "Of course I'm with you. But it's hard to believe they're the same people in this picture. So much has changed in the last ten years. It makes me sad."

Bonnie reached across the table and patted his hand. "I know what you mean. Are we heading down the same path?"

"I don't want to think about it." Ralph drained his coffee cup and pushed himself away from the table.

Bonnie turned at the sound of footsteps in the hallway. She knew it was her father, now up for the day and probably looking for his coffee and toast—the same breakfast he'd eaten for the past 50 years. Her mother, Jean, would soon follow. Bonnie knew her mom was devoted to looking after her husband now that his memory was slipping and he wasn't as steady on his feet as he used to be.

Bonnie noticed her dad seemed agitated. She hoped she could communicate with him enough to calm him down. She worried that he wouldn't recognize her. One day he'd call her Bonnie, and the next he'd call her Olive, the name of his older sister, whom he'd always loved and looked up to. Sure enough, today Bonnie was "Olive" to her dad.

"Olive! Olive!" he called. Bonnie could tell he was frantic with worry.

"I'm here." She met him in the hall and linked her arm in his. "Right this way. Your coffee and toast are ready."

Ben shook his head and waved her away, nearly smacking Bonnie in the face, though it was clear he didn't know what he was doing.

"What is it? You look frightened." She helped him into a chair.

"There was a strange woman in bed with me. Nearly scared the daylights out of me. Get her out of here! What will your mother think?"

Bonnie covered her mouth to keep from laughing out loud. "That's your wife and my mom, Jean. The same woman you've been married to for 63 years."

"I don't believe it. She looks different. Jean has blond hair and blue eyes. She doesn't wear glasses, and she's skinny too."

Just then Bonnie saw her mother come around the corner and into the kitchen. Bonnie hoped her mom hadn't heard her father's hurtful remark.

"What'd I tell you, Olive!" Ben shouted when Jean sat down next to him. "Now will you believe me?" He pointed to the stranger. "This woman has gray hair and glasses and she's plump."

Bonnie grabbed her mother's trembling hand and squeezed it. "Daddy's teasing." She hoped to ease the tension in the room, but it didn't work.

Jean looked at Bonnie and then at Ben. "He's right," she said and chuckled. "I don't know this man, and he doesn't know me. My husband has brown hair, a mustache, gray eyes, and strong muscles."

Bonnie cracked up. Ralph broke out laughing, and Bonnie's parents joined in.

Ralph winked at Bonnie. "Looks like we have some shopping to do."

"Shopping?" Bonnie wondered if her husband was losing it too. What did shopping have to do with her parents' confusion?

He patted his back pocket, which held his wallet. "We'll have to buy separate beds for these two and put them in different rooms. Can't have strangers sleeping with one another in our house."

Bonnie let out a sigh and smiled. It wouldn't be easy, but with Ralph at her side she could handle anything—even the surprising and sometimes amusing changes in her parents.

Reflection

My flesh and my heart may fail, but God is the
strength of my heart and my portion forever
(Psalm 73:26).

———————

I love you, Lord, and I know you love me. Thank you for being with me in the trials and triumphs of life.

Poppy's Girlfriend

L eonard offered to watch his granddaughter one Saturday afternoon while his wife, Lou, attended a movie with their daughter, Ann. Five-year-old Jenny hopped out of the car when her mother pulled into the driveway and ran into Poppy's waiting arms.

The two waved goodbye as Lou and Ann backed out while blowing kisses their way. Poppy led Jenny into the house where he laid out a game of Fairyland, two PB & J sandwiches, and carrot sticks for a picnic in the yard. Fresh lemonade made with lemons from Poppy's tree and chocolate-crisp cookies Nana Lou had made that morning were waiting on the outdoor table.

Jenny skipped ahead. "Isn't this fun, Poppy? It's just the two of us. We don't have anyone telling us what to do."

Poppy Leonard winked and smiled. "I kinda like that too," he agreed.

After lunch and the game, Poppy and Jenny walked around the block two times and then stopped at the park where Jenny pushed Poppy on the big kids' swing and he pushed her on the one for little kids. They both slid down the slide together, and Poppy chased Jenny through the play tunnel.

They arrived home at four. Poppy plopped in a chair. He was

pooped. But not Jenny. She wanted to play some more. "How about we look at some pictures?" he asked. "That's a nice, quiet activity. We can rest at the same time."

Jenny pulled a fat album out of the cabinet under the TV and opened it. "I don't remember these pictures," she said. "Are they new?"

Poppy leaned forward. "No, they're old." He pointed to a photo of a little boy. "That's me when I was a young lad about your age, and that's my cousin George standing next to me."

Jenny looked back and forth from the photos to Poppy. She wrinkled her nose and rolled her eyes.

"Is it hard to think of me as a little boy?" asked Poppy.

"Yeah. And it's hard to think of me as a big lady."

Poppy laughed. "Well, that's quite a few years away so you don't have to think about it yet."

The door opened and Lou and Ann walked in.

"What's up, you two?" Ann asked.

Jenny held up the album. "We're looking at pictures of Poppy when he was little."

"Oh my," Lou commented. "We haven't opened that book for a long time."

"Then maybe you don't remember the picture of the pretty lady," Jenny responded.

"What pretty lady?" asked Lou. "Maybe it was my mother. She was beautiful."

Jenny pointed to a young woman in a bathing suit standing next to Poppy at the beach when he was a teenager. "No, this one," she said. "Poppy, was that your girlfriend?"

"Sure was!" Poppy agreed. He smiled and nudged Lou with an elbow.

"Did you know Poppy had a girlfriend?" Jenny asked Nana Lou.

"Sure did," said Lou. "I'm the girlfriend!"

Jenny's eyes grew wide. "No you're not! You're Poppy's wife."

Poppy had some explaining to do, and Lou left it entirely up to him.

Reflection

If any of you lacks wisdom,
he should ask God (James 1:5).

———————

*Dear God, you are with me even in sticky situations. I'm sure
glad about that.*

Cool It!

Neda and Bill decided to throw a party to celebrate their fortieth wedding anniversary. Neda wanted to make a big fuss. After all, she'd put up with Bill all these years. She felt she deserved roses and applause and a large gathering of friends.

Bill, on the other hand, preferred a quiet affair—just a few neighbors and their son and family. *No need to broadcast the event to the world,* he thought. *They were married, that's all. Why the big deal? Millions of couples all over the world were married. A simple toast would do, a few laughs, some conversation, and early to bed as usual.*

Neda, hands on her hips, stared down at her husband as he proposed something so boring and mundane. Later she waved him off as he passed her on the terrace. She continued on with her list and her plans for refreshments, beverages, and even a few games. Maybe she'd even ask their neighbor Manny to play the piano or guitar. There was room out back for couples to dance. Wouldn't that be a lovely addition to the festivities?

Neda presented her plan to Bill over dinner that evening. He rolled his eyes as only he could do. He threw up his hands. "Neda, I surrender!"

"It's about time," she quipped. "I've been waiting to hear that for 40 years."

Bill grabbed Neda by the hand and twirled her around the dining room till she was dizzy. He pulled her down on the living room sofa and planted a big smooch on her cheek. "I may not be the most romantic guy in the world," he said, "but I've loved you all these years and I still do. You'll always be my bride."

Neda was suddenly at a loss for words—the first time in a long time. She didn't know what to say or do so she simply took in what her husband had said. He'd loved her all these years and still did. He just didn't always show it. She sank back into the flowered cushion and smiled.

"Let's toast ourselves," said Bill. "We don't need a bunch of people around to celebrate our marriage." He filled two glasses with crushed ice and sparkling apple cider. Then he raised his glass to his bride and quipped, "I only have 'ice' for you! And don't you know you're the 'apple' of my eye."

Then Bill did a most unexpected thing. He pulled out two passes for Disneyland. "Forget the party," he said. "We're going away for the weekend by ourselves. We're gonna be two kids again—now that we're in our second childhood."

Neda burst out laughing and hugged her groom of 40 years.

Reflection

May your fountain be blessed, and may you rejoice
in the wife of your youth (Proverbs 5:18).

Dear God, spending time with the one I love is one of the great blessings of my life. And spending time with you makes all the rest possible. Thank you for that.

A Good, Swift Kick

Poke was nearly at his wit's end with his wife, Shirl. She just didn't get it! He was working as fast as he could, but it was never fast enough to satisfy her. As soon as he finished one project she had another lined up. Her list was as long as the menu at Shorty's Fast-Food Palace:

» Paint Laurie's dollhouse.

» Fix the broken shutter.

» Change the oil in the van.

» Plant bulbs now for next year's flowers.

» Send Nadia a birthday card.

» Shovel the mound of dirt in the yard.

» Take Skippy to the vet.

These items covered an entire page because beneath each one Shirl listed specific details, such as "be sure the vet cuts Skippy's nails" or "pick a card that isn't too flowery. You know how Nadia can be." Shirl also color-coded them. Green meant "right now." Yellow stood for "complete within 24 hours." There were more, but Poke couldn't keep 'em all straight. Next thing he knew she'd add another order to the list: "Memorize my color codes," and it would be in red.

Poke walked into the kitchen from the garage, wiped his sweaty brow, and grabbed a cool drink from the fridge. He thought about reminding his wife that he'd just turned 70, and he had a right to slow down. Not that it would do any good. She'd come back at him with some smart-alecky remark like, "All the more reason to get going. You don't have much time to finish the list."

Shirl walked in just as Poke took the last swig of his lemon-lime soda.

"No wonder your mom called you Poke. You're pokey, that's what." She let out a deep sigh and pulled a paper from her pocket. "I'd like to go over a few things before I leave for town."

Poke sat up. "Go over a few things? That's it? Just go over them… or do you mean me to do them?"

The cold look in Shirl's eyes told Poke she didn't appreciate his humor. "You know what I mean. Go over and then do!"

A funny image crossed Poke's mind—Shirl in Native American dress from the Wild West days: long, black braids; feathers in her hair; moccasins on her feet; and a long, animal-skin dress. Suddenly he broke out laughing. He decided to take a chance—and inject a bit of humor into this humorless conversation. "Shirl, if you were a squaw back in the Old West your name would be 'Kick in the Pants.'" That tickled Poke so much he doubled over.

But Shirl remained upright and got in the last word, as always. Without missing a beat she shot back, "And if you were the squaw's husband, your name would be 'Needs Kick in the Pants.'"

Reflection

His God instructs him and teaches
him the right way (Isaiah 28:26).

---

*Dear God, you may feel I need a good, swift kick sometimes,
but instead you love me. Thank you!*

Hey, Good Lookin'

Jody was proud of her husband. Carl was a gentleman in every way. And he was a good-lookin' dude as well, and even more so at age 65. He had a full head of gray hair, flat belly, and well-manicured hands. He was also a great dresser. She loved being on his arm and letting everyone know she was his spouse.

Carl was a salesman in men's suits at a prominent department store. He had a great eye for fashion and helped many men find just the right clothes for work and leisure. The saleswomen also admired Carl. He always had a kind and encouraging word whenever he ran into them in the aisles or at a staff meeting. And he was good at remembering their names.

One young woman named Mindy was especially attentive to Carl and even sought him out from time to time in the lunchroom when they had a few moments to talk. She asked his advice whenever she was having problems with her boyfriend.

Jody heard about this from time to time and noticed it made her uncomfortable. *How silly!* she told herself. *Mindy's a twenty-something. There's nothing to worry about. Carl and I have been married 40 years, and we've been faithful to one another the entire time.*

Carl never failed to compliment Jody on her appearance, and after an evening out he'd often say, "You were the prettiest one at the ball. No one is fairer than you." She felt like Cinderella and Carl was her prince charming.

One Tuesday evening after work Carl bounded in the door happy, smiling, and almost giddy. *What's with him?* Jody wondered. They enjoyed a quiet supper on the patio, and as they lingered over coffee Carl began talking about Mindy...about how cute she was and how many problems the poor girl had with her boyfriend, Bill. "This guy just doesn't get what a special lady he has. Why, any man would be proud to be in a relationship with her."

Jody felt her pulse jump and her palms were suddenly wet. She started to talk and then stopped, afraid she'd say the wrong thing and sound like a jealous wife. But maybe she was jealous. As she stood up to clear the dishes, Carl continued.

"Today I spoke with Mindy for just a minute or two while we passed in the cosmetics aisle. As we said goodbye she reached over and pinched my cheek. I didn't know what to do. I probably turned as red as that tomato," he said, pointing to one in a basket on the windowsill.

Jody was all ears. She had to hear the rest of this story!

"Mindy told me how much I'd helped her over the last few months with my sage advice and kindness. Just as I puffed up with pride that such a cute young thing would even notice me, she leaned in and whispered, 'Carl, you're adorable. You remind me of my grandpa.' With that she waved and smiled and off she went." Carl slumped his shoulders. "I came down to earth really fast. The Lord says something about pride going before we fall, right?" Carl looked at Jody. "What do you think of that? Pretty funny, hmmm?"

Jody had only one thing on her mind. "What department does she work in? I'm going to give her all my business from now on. And I'll introduce myself as Grandma—Carl's wife."

Reflection

Do not lie to each other, since you have taken off
your old self with its practices and have put on the
new self (Colossians 3:9).

---

*Lord, I'm always surprised when I have a burst of jealousy. I
don't want it but still it's there. Thank you for restoring my
perspective and helping me remember that with your grace
to guide me I have nothing to fear.*

Wise Investment?

Toni fell in love with Rex, a fine-looking man she'd met on a cruise for singles. She hadn't planned to marry again after her husband, Arnold, died but when she sat next to Rex at dinner one night on the ship, she knew something special was happening between them. They talked till 11 o'clock that night about family, grandkids, former spouses—he was a widower—and hobbies. They shared the same faith walk too. This seemed too good to be true. Then Toni hit a stumbling block: age. Rex was 15 years older than she was. He was 78 and Toni was 63. Hmmm. She worried that if they got serious with one another, they'd have only a short time together and then she'd be a widow—again.

Still, she reasoned, *weren't even a few years together better than none? There were no guarantees at any age, so why hold back?* Toni talked herself into continuing the relationship when the cruise ended and seeing where the Lord would lead them. Rex agreed. He admitted he only had eyes for Toni, and he hoped she'd believe that he would take good care of her till God called him home.

The couple married six months later, and their friends and family heralded their union. Everyone commented on how well suited they were to one another. Shortly after their honeymoon, Rex shared an important personal detail. He had been having dental problems for the past three years and was in considerable pain from time to time. He'd put off doing anything drastic—like wearing dentures—yet he wasn't sure he could put up with the discomfort much longer.

Toni suggested they see his dentist and ask his opinion.

"Buy yourself some new teeth," advised Dr. Gregory. "I know it's an expensive proposition, but Rex, think of how it will change the quality of your life—and Toni's too."

That was enough to convince Rex to fork over the $10,000. "A wise investment," he declared. "Don't know why I waited so long."

The following week, on Tuesday morning, the process was underway. Rex would soon be pain-free even if it did mean having to wear false teeth. That morning after Toni dropped Rex at the dental clinic, she went off to play tennis with her friend Grace. After a set the women stopped for a water break. Toni confided the whole "teeth" story to her friend. Grace thought it was a great idea, and she congratulated Toni on supporting her new husband.

Toni frowned. "But Rex is 78 years old. He thinks this is a wise investment, but I'm not sure. When I consider Rex's present age versus his life expectancy, I don't think there's a financial counselor on the planet who would advise us to shell out 10K with no return. But then I don't want him to be in pain. And going out with someone toothless doesn't seem too appealing. It's only money, I guess."

Reflection

Each man's life is but a breath (Psalm 39:5).

Dear Lord, the only truly worthwhile investment is the one I have with you—for eternity—because of what Jesus did on the cross for me. I am so grateful!

Lady's Man

Mac transferred the bacon slices from the grill to a paper towel and patted them dry. He stirred the scrambled eggs, added a dash of salt and pepper, and cut up some green onion to sprinkle on top. "The answer is a big fat no." He turned to his wife and frowned. "Cheri, I did my time in the pen and I'm finished. They need to get that."

Cheri laughed. Mac referred to his work on the Homeowners Association Board in their previous community as "doing time in the pen." She couldn't blame him. He had worked hard at the thankless task for three years.

"Enough with volunteering," he said on his last day in office. "I'm retired now and I'm going to enjoy myself. Let some youngster take over. These kids think they know everything anyway. Let 'em prove it."

But here they were in a new community—this time exclusively for seniors—so there weren't any know-it-all young people to do the job. The homeowners wanted to get organized, and they needed someone to take charge—someone who knew how to do it. Word had gotten around that Mac was their man. He began receiving calls and emails begging him to run for president. The latest one had come that morning from Rick, who lived around the corner from Mac and Cheri.

Mac snapped a napkin into his lap as he and Cheri sat down to eat. He mumbled something about how he was no longer available for phone calls unless it was from one of their grown kids. He barely got the words out of his mouth when his cell phone went off. He yanked it off his belt and handed it to Cheri.

"Hello, Cheri speaking," she said. Then she handed it over to Mac. "I think you'll want to take this one."

"Mac speaking." Mac noticed the tone in his own voice soften. He couldn't control it. Annie was so sweet, and she obviously wasn't trying to badger him. She simply needed his advice.

Cheri folded her hands in her lap and leaned over. Mac could tell she wanted in on this conversation. He held out the phone so she could hear too.

Mac listened a little longer. A smile cracked his lips. Then he felt himself grinning and nodding. "All three of you? Hmmm. Interesting offer. I see your point. You're right about that. I do have more experience than anyone, and..."

Cheri pulled away and sat back in her chair, arms crossed in front of her chest.

"I'll give it some thought and get back to you tomorrow. How's that?" Mac nodded and clicked the cell phone shut. Cheri stared at him with a knowing look in her eye, the one he'd seen often in their 45 years of marriage.

"Annie, Cynthia, and Lena will be your righthand gals if you take the job, right?"

"How did you know?"

"Because I put them up to it."

"You what?"

"Let's face it, Mac. You're ideal for the job. You won't listen to me, so I decided to sic the ladies on you. They all want to be on the board, but they need a strong, knowledgeable man to help. I can't imagine anyone being stronger or more suited to the job than you, dear. Besides, you're a ladies' man, at heart. You like to rescue damsels in distress!"

Mac nuzzled Cheri's neck. "I'm only one lady's man," he whispered. "All right I'll do it—for you and for us."

Reflection

God is not unjust; he will not forget your work and
the love you have shown him as you have helped his
people and continue to help them (Hebrews 6:10).

———————

*Lord, thank you for giving me the security of my everlasting
relationship with you. I am your friend, and you are mine.*

Karen O'Connor

*Opening hearts and connecting lives
through writing and speaking*

Karen has authored many magazine articles and more than 50 books, including *Walkin' with God Ain't for Wimps* and *Gettin' Old Ain't for Wimps* (more than 200,000 copies sold). Her numerous awards include the Paul A. Witty Award for short story writing (International Reading Association, 2005), the Special Recognition Award (Mount Hermon Christian Writers Conference, 2002), and Writer of the Year (San Diego Christian Writers Guild, 1997).

A sought-after speaker, Karen uses humor to inspire people to...

» experience and express more joy and gratitude

» influence and inspire for positive growth

» achieve greater intimacy with God, self, and others

» polish communication and leadership skills

She speaks at businesses, schools, churches, and community organizations, and she's a frequent guest on national radio and television programs, including *Faith at Work, Coast-to-Coast, Lifestyle Magazine,* and *The 700 Club.*

For more information contact:

Karen O'Connor Communications
10 Pajaro Vista Court
Watsonville, CA 95076

Phone: 831-768-7335
Email: Karen@KarenOconnor.com

If you enjoyed reading
The Golden Years Ain't for Wimps,
you'll also get a kick out of...

Walkin' with God Ain't for Wimps

*Take a few minutes to relax and enjoy
these treasured, funny moments of life.
You'll be glad you did!*

Through amusing stories that touch the heart and soul, humorist Karen O'Connor reveals the joy, strength, and laughter that is ours when we walk with God—regardless of our circumstances. These short, real-life vignettes will have you chuckling as you relate to the adventures and foibles of people just like you—or someone you know—and then share them with family and friends.

Each delightful, easy-to-read tale concludes with an insightful Scripture and simple, life-affirming prayer that will remind you that God is with you in all ways—always!

Gettin' Old
Ain't for Wimps

Bursting with wit and wisdom, these lighthearted, real-life stories, insightful scriptures, and heartfelt prayers will make you chuckle and confess "That sounds just like me!" Popular speaker and author Karen O'Connor invites you to celebrate the joys and misadventures of getting older. Have you noticed that...

- when you can't find your glasses, they're usually on your head?
- the delightful honesty of youth sometimes bites?
- love still makes your heart skip a beat...or two...or three?

Are you ready to trade in your wimp status for a more courageous existence? Or are you still wondering what lies ahead? *Gettin' Old Ain't for Wimps* hilariously affirms that life will always be filled with wonder, promise, and adventure!

Gettin' Old Still Ain't for Wimps

Laughter truly is the best medicine for those of us approaching middle or—dare we say it?—old age. Packed with tongue-in-cheek humor, hilarious misunderstandings, and funny foibles, *Gettin' Old Still Ain't for Wimps* will make you smile and remind you how great life can be. From ordering a Coke and fries at the bank drive-thru to having to admit your age to get a senior discount, these stories reveal that...

- beauty begins with a good heart
- shaking things up is not just for the young
- lost and found becomes a way of life after 50
- love happens at all ages
- laughter is contagious

With inspirational reflections and lively prayers, this great collection of anecdotes will tickle your funny bone and make getting on in years more enjoyable.